THOUGHT CATALOG BOOKS

Single AF

Single AF

The Trials And Triumphs Of Living Solo

BECCA MARTIN

Thought Catalog Books

Brooklyn, NY

Contents

1

To The Girl That They Love After Your Break Up

I used to hate you when I had no reason to. I hated you because you became the new me.

You filled the void I left in his heart. You took my place in his life. You were lying next to him in bed and receiving his handwritten love notes. You were holding his hand on long drives down the back roads. You were standing in his kitchen talking to his family, laughing with them over dinner. You were running through the woods with his dog.

You were everything I once was, maybe even more.

You might not have replaced me completely, but he's not alone.

I told myself you weren't as pretty as me. I told myself you weren't as good for him as I was. I told myself you weren't capable of loving him like I did. I told myself everything I could think of to try to make myself feel better about losing him to you. I said every horrible thing I could think of because somehow I felt that was going to make me feel better, even though I knew it wasn't going to change anything. I placed bets with my friends on how long your rebound would last.

Because that's what it was, right? It was just a rebound.

We just broke up, how could he possibly love you? Maybe

not love, but how could he kiss you? How could he talk to you the way he talked to me?

How could he go from being as comfortable as we were together to starting over and learning your flaws? Learning your strengths and weaknesses? Learning what keeps you up at night and what makes your heart ache? How could he do that?

I couldn't move from bed. I couldn't eat dinner. I couldn't look at my family in the face. I didn't want to be around anyone. I didn't want to do anything.

I hated myself for breaking up with him because he went to you. He turned to you in a time when I would have turned to him.

But you were comforting him now while I had no one.

He turned to you over our evaporating love story. I know he did, because I was that girl for him when he broke up with the girl he loved before he loved me.

I hated myself for that. I hated myself for doing that to his ex before me. Now I understand the misery she must have been feeling when she started seeing pictures of him and me together. When she started hearing my name associated with his…because I'm at the other end of the spectrum now.

Life has an interesting, twisted way of putting us through the epitome of karma, of showing us that the hurt we put unto others will soon enough be the pain inflicted unto ourselves.

I think I started hating him for that. How could he do that again? He went from his ex,to me to you almost as if it was a continuous chain reaction. He went one to the other with no time to live life on his own, to figure out what he really needed.

Now time has passed. My wounds aren't as deep; they've merely healed themselves completely over time. I don't hate you anymore, I don't think you're ugly, and I don't think I'm better for him than you.

Because I'm not.

I'm not the same girl he fell in love with anymore.

I hope you love him, because one of us has to and I'm too far gone for him now.

2

9 Things You Need To Know Before Dating The Girl Who Has Always Been Single

1. She is her own person.

You aren't her other half; she is her own whole person. She doesn't need you to hold her hand when she crosses the street, she doesn't need you to buy her things just because she's interested in them, and she doesn't need you checking up on her every minute of the day. But that doesn't mean she won't ever want you too, she just used to doing everything on her own.

2. She has an incredible support system.

She hasn't had to focus her time on anyone specific so she invests it into her friends and family. She always lends a hand when they need and is there for them, just like they are for her. By coming into her life you are added to her endless loving support system, but you are not the base of it.

3. She is a passionate and dedicated person.

Being single has led her to so many amazing opportunities that she has been able to focus her time on. Whether it is work, a hobby, a sport, or something that just makes her happy, she has a passion for whatever "it" is. You can't expect her to give it up now just because you're in her life. If you're in her life, it's because she wants you there so she will work on the balance and sharing her passion with you.

4. Her love was never limited.

She loves so much, even before you. She has her family and friends, co-workers and pets—even if it's not the romantic love she was never limited. She loves her life and that fills her heart, but she will always make room for new love because love is not limited.

5. She doesn't need to be saved.

She doesn't need you to swoop into her life and be her knight in shining armor. She has been on her own long enough to know how to do things for herself. Don't try to overpower her and treat her like she needs help with everything because it won't turn out in your favor.

6. She's worried about pushing you away.

She's had plenty of people come into her life and leave unannounced. She might have feelings about certain things that she will compress until she is more comfortable around you because she doesn't want to turn you off.

7. She understands relationships, the good, the bad and the ugly.

She might not have been in many relationships, but that doesn't mean she doesn't know anything about them. Her friends come to her for everything. She's seen her friends cry over their significant others cheating and she's seen her friends smile ear to ear over the nice thing their significant others did. She's also seen her friends go through the unnecessary drama of relationships that should have been over months ago. Just because she isn't in her own relationships doesn't mean she doesn't understand what they should and shouldn't be like.

8. She enjoys her alone time.

She's used to spending time on her own, it's not a bad thing, it's just become her comfort. Don't take it personally if she wants to spend a night by herself, she just isn't used to being with someone all the time.

9. She doesn't want to rush things.

She knows too well what it feels like to have someone there, then before she knows it they're gone. She wants to make sure that she ready for you and you're ready for her. She might be hesitant at first, but if you're serious then she will start showing you her love.

3

I Only Want You When It's 2 AM

I only want you when it's 2 AM, never when it's 2 PM. I only want you when I have to walk home alone at night and I'm scared of the way the world has become. I only want you when I watch a creepy episode of *How To Get Away With Murder* so I don't have to sleep alone with fear. I only want you when my roommates are gone for the night and I hear a creepy noise in my house, and for some reason I would feel safer with you around.

I only want you when I'm tossing and turning, wide awake looking for someone to talk to because no matter how many times I put down my phone and put my pillow over my head, I still can't sleep. I only want you when it's cold in my room and I want a warm body next to me, to wrap my legs around and share body heat. I only want you when it's convenient for me, and it's only convenient at 2 AM.

I don't want to try to slide out of bed without trying to wake you up in the morning. I don't want you in the morning when I'm making breakfast for one. I don't want you in the morning when I'm trying to get ready for work. I don't want to have to say the awkward goodbyes when I'm trying to rush out the door.

I don't want to look at my phone and wonder if you'll text me. I don't want to be hopeful that you'll miss me because I really don't want to miss you. I don't want the cycle of games to begin that relationships have now evolved too.

So no matter how much I might want you at 2 AM, I won't give in to you.

No matter how many nights you text me asking me what I'm doing, I won't answer because I'll never want you in the morning.

The way I want you is to stay hidden behind the closure of my bedroom door. I don't want the world to know about you…about us. As much as I want you, it will never be enough, because no matter what I'll never want you in the morning.

There is an uneasiness about 2 AM that makes you think things you wouldn't think at 2 PM. There is a comfort in the day: being busy, being around friends and family, and having the sun shining on your skin. But the darkness brings different feelings, darker ones. It traps you with your thoughts, makes you feel useless, maybe worthless. It makes you feel alone more than anything and no one likes feeling alone.

I hate feeling alone.

But the sun will rise again; the sun will always rise again. The day will start over and you will realize that things are not as bad as they seem at 2 AM when you're trapped with your own thoughts. Things will be OK again because you do matter; you're not worthless and you're not alone. No one can fix those feelings at 2 AM except you. That is why I don't give into you at 2 AM because when the morning comes I will wake up and I will realize that I never needed you.

4

I Want An Every Day Kind Of Love

I want a Monday kind of love.

The kind where you both roll over and pull yourselves out of bed for work, tired and groggy, but sit at the table to drink your morning coffee together. Partially dreading the five long days ahead of you, but also excited for a fresh start and the chance to get so much accomplished. You say your goodbyes as you run out the door and head in opposite directions. Losing each other in your rearview mirrors, but knowing you will see each other again soon.

I want a Tuesday kind of love.

The kind love that is directionless. You don't know where the week will take you, but you're still going forward. A Tuesday kind of love is reality. It's not rolling out of bed on a Monday morning, still groggy from the weekend. It's paying the bills, running errands, and ordering take out. It's conversation about what your boss did and what's expected of you this week. It's looking at each other and saying, "We can do this."

I want a Wednesday kind of love.

The kind that feels like we've almost made it but we're in a rut. It's the kind of day that tests you, the day that shows your strengths and weaknesses. It's the excitement of closing in on the end of the week with the history of Monday and Tuesday behind us. It's the kind of love where you dance around the kitchen making dinner together and sing along to your favorite songs.

I want a Thursday kind of love.

Thursday is a date night kind of night. The week is almost behind you and the weekend is nearly here. A Thursday love is comfortable; you've made it through the rough stuff already. A Thursday love is a deeper kind of love. It says *You're almost there; just one more day then you have freedom.* A Thursday kind of love ties up loose ends while leading you straight to new beginnings.

I want a Friday kind of love.

The love that is fun, the love you yearn for. A Friday kind of love is the feeling of having endless possibilities and opportunities. You never know what the weekend could bring, but you're always filled with hope for the best. A Friday kind of love that your morning coffee will be matched with happy hour beers. Filled with co-workers and friends. The kind of day where anything could happen, but either way you are happy and you are thankful.

I want a Saturday kind of love.

A love that is busy or relaxed. You can make the day whatever you choose. You can sit on your porch and drink your morning coffee before going on a walk through the neighborhood or heading to morning yoga. A Saturday kind of love is all that it's cracked up to be. You have the freedom to go to a wine festival or go to a friend's house to watch the big game. A Saturday love is whatever you make it out to be, but it's always together.

I want a Sunday kind of love, the best kind of love.

The kind of love where you roll over in the morning and have nothing scheduled all day. You can lie in bed until noon or wake up and cuddle on the couch watching endless episodes of Netflix. A Sunday kind of love feels effortless; it's not the Tuesday kind of love where reality hits you. A Sunday love feels like home. Waking up tangled in sheets together, looking into each other's eyes. Laughing about what Saturday night might have brought. A Sunday love feels invincible, even though you know Monday is right around the corner. A Sunday love is beautiful, just like every other day of the week.

5

You Cannot Chase Someone Who Does Not Want To Be Caught

If a someone wants you they will make it known.

They will answer your texts, maybe not right away because they have a life (which is a good thing). But they won't constantly and consistently leave you hanging. They will come over and hang out with you and your friends when you ask them to. They will be in your life. They will make an effort. No one, for the most part, is that complicated. There are the exceptions, there are always exceptions, but for the most part if someone is interested in you they will make an effort and if not, you need to quit wasting your time.

Trying harder to get the guy or the girl generally won't make your relationship progress any further because more times than not it will be a major turn off. But it is the *same* for men and women.

If they want to be with you they will make it known. They will text you back, they will respond to you. Instead of letting you double text over and over, they'll speak up. They will come over and hang out with you when you invite them, and they will make an effort to make you feel important.

As humans we always crave attention from those who don't give us attention.

The saying "Who cares less has more power" is accurate because the one who cares less won't get their heart broken and they won't be made a fool of.

When your heart is involved you do stupid things, even like trying to convince yourself to continue pursing someone you have no business pursuing.

The signs are basically laid out for you. You can tell your best friend to stop texting that bitch or that asshole because you know they are wasting their time and you don't want to see them get hurt. You know they are more emotionally invested into the "relationship" and you know it isn't going to work out in their favor. You can see clearly because your heart isn't on the line.

But it's so much easier said than done when it comes to your heart.

It's hard to take your own advice in that case because you think that maybe if you try hard enough you will be the exception; you will be the one who changes them and you can steal their heart. But realistically you won't win them over; you're just another person to keep them busy or foolishly annoy them.

Don't stay when you know you should leave. Don't beg for the emotional investment of someone who doesn't want you and please; don't beg for love. Don't continue to text him when he hasn't answered your last three messages. Don't ask her to hang out when she has declined your last few invitations because if she wants to hang out, she will ask you. Stop holding on to people who are already twenty steps ahead of you and not looking back.

Aside from the rare exception, no one is chasing you down after realizing they just let you slip from their naïve little finger tips. Life isn't a romantic movie; no one is running to the airport to get on the same plane as you. No one is showing up at your doorsteps with a poetic apology about how stupid they were to let you go.

Don't place your self worth in the palms on someone who has no intentions of sticking around when you fall, and more importantly, don't chase after them.

6

The Truth Is, I Don't Love Myself Enough To Let You Love Me Yet

I look in the mirror and I hate what I see.

I've hated it for years now.

I grab and pull at my skin imagining how much better I would feel about myself if I just put down the beer and started working out more. I get angry and frustrated with myself. I point out flaw after flaw on myself. **All I see looking back at me is rejection.** All I feel is hate and regret, and I can't stop the feelings.

I don't love myself.

I tell myself over and over that I am the one in control of my body and my choices. I tell myself to choose better next time around, but I fail. I look forward to the girl I want to be. I think of all the ways my life would get better if I was more fit. I know that might not be true; I'll always find flaws, but it would be better for me. Or at least that is what I keep telling myself.

Because maybe, just *maybe*, if I loved myself, even a little bit, that would allow me to let you love me, too.

I finally think I've found the source of my self-inflicting pain. I've found the reasoning behind why I won't let anyone in. It's because I don't love myself and I'm too self-conscious to let anyone else love me.

I hate my arms because they're not slim. I hate my stomach because it isn't toned and firm. I hate my hands and feet because they're big. I hate my skin because I'm 22 and still have acne like my teenage self.

I don't know how anyone could love me, so I push them away.

I push them away from me sexually because I'm scared they won't want me once they see me naked. I push them away because I don't see how they could possibly find me attractive. I push them away because I don't have any confidence in myself, so I'd rather not allow them to compliment me or adore me when I would question them constantly.

I'm admitting that I don't love myself, and this is something I've been trying to suppress for a while now. I've been trying to hide it away under lock and key.

I've been busy telling myself that I like being single and I just don't like anyone who likes me. But the truth is, I haven't given anyone a chance because I'm scared they will reject me for not being thin enough, or fit enough, or toned enough because those are all reasons I reject myself. Even if they tell me those are all things they love about me, I convince myself they're lying.

I push people away from me in a romantic and sexual way. I compare myself to others. **I think I'm not good enough because I could always be better.** I know it isn't healthy, but I've finally admitted it; I've finally said that I don't allow myself to be loved because I don't love myself.

I don't want anyone to love me until I love myself first.

I don't want someone to come into my life and try to fix the broken pieces of me. I don't want someone to come and shower me in compliments hoping to lift my self-esteem. I don't want someone to try to heal my open wounds. **I want to fix myself on my own time; I *need* to fix myself on my own time because once I love myself then maybe I'll let you love me.**

Until then, I'll be busy working on me.

7

Date The Guy Who Texts At 2:30 AM To See If You Got Home Safe (Not The One Who Booty Calls You)

You texted me at 2:30 AM and I was expecting a booty call, but I should have known you better than that. It's just been so long since you've texted me late at night, I was mostly taken by surprise.

You used to text me about plans and deep thoughts when we weren't together, but now I didn't know where your "hi" was going. But all your "hi" led to was "I just wanted to make sure you got home safely."

You didn't push for anything. You didn't hint at coming over. You didn't mention hooking up or hanging out. You simply followed your genuine statement with "goodnight." And that was it.

Sometimes I find myself wondering why we aren't together. You're funny and kind and caring, but our stars were never aligned. God must have not had it in his plans for us to end up together. I don't believe we're supposed to end up together, either. We gave it our best college try, but that's all it was, a college try.

I still remember all the good morning texts you would send me when I didn't wake up by your side to kiss you good morning. I still remember all the late night trips you'd make after you'd get out of work so neither of us would have to sleep alone. I still remember how'd you'd always set your phone alarm for me to get up for work in case mine didn't go off. You'd even leave it set when I wasn't there because you knew I'd need it the next day we were together. I still remember looking forward to seeing you, talking to you, being with you. Of everything I remember about us, it's that we knew we weren't meant to be together.

We each knew in our hearts we couldn't be together. We just weren't compatible for each other, no matter how much either of us wanted it. Our lives were heading in different directions and we accepted that. For us it was for the best.

Even though our match made in heaven went straight to hell you taught me a thing or two.

You taught me to keep in mind the guy who texts you at 2:30 AM. Not the one who texts "u up?" and wants to sleep with you. Not the one who asks you to Netflix and chill. Not the one who only texts you when he can't go home with anyone else at the bar. Those aren't the guys you want to be with.

Date the guy who cares enough to text you at 2:30 AM to make sure you got home safely. Date the guy who cares about you as a person, not just someone who cares only when it's beneficial to him. Date the guy who understands the importance of treating you properly, even after they've had a few drinks at the bar. Date the guy who doesn't flirt with everyone that lays eyes on him, but only has eyes for you.

Date the guy who put you before himself, because you'd do the same for him. Date the guy who gives and not just takes, but also reciprocate that for him. Date the guy who makes you happy and doesn't make you feel like you're constantly begging for his attention.

Even though our love failed, what I learned from you was important. Date someone who makes sure you're safe at home when the rest of the world is worried about finding a body to go home with. That's the kind of person you want to spend forever with.

8

This Is Why We Can't Let Go Of People Who Aren't Good For Us (Even Though We Should)

I knew from the start you were "that asshole" but I have a comical way of thinking that I can be the one to impact someone, to change them. I naïvely think I will make a difference, so I attempt it. I try to be the one who lets them in, the one who gives them chance after chance to prove to me they aren't a bad person.

You were slightly different. The guy I met three years ago isn't the same guy I know now. The guy I know now has a sweet side but has a hard time showing it. He doesn't like to expose his emotions. He covers them up at all cost. It's been three years and I still can't figure out why.

I can't figure out what it is about you that keeps me around, either. I put 120 percent into the relationship while you put in a mere 40 to 50 percent on a good day. But I still stay hanging around.

I keep holding on. I keep telling myself things will get better, that you do care about me. I tell myself that you have a hard time showing affection. I tell myself that you show you care about me in different ways, even though I'm not entirely sure what those ways are. I keep twisting things in my head because I didn't want to accept not having you in my life.

I should have known by the way you would only make time for me when it was convenient for you. I should have known when you didn't want me to know the little personal details of your life that I so openly shared with you. I should have known that you really didn't care when I'd invite you to dinners, parties, or even my own house and you always treated it like a chore. I should have known especially when you wouldn't come based off who else would be there.

I had hoped over and over again. I hoped that maybe if I opened up to you, you would in turn open up to me. Instead I just kept making a fool of myself; I kept opening up for you to not even respond, time and time again. Maybe it wasn't even that you didn't have any stories you wanted to share, maybe they weren't your stories to tell. But instead of not reciprocating with your own words, you would simply disregard me. I would maybe get a head nod, a couple words, maybe a look, and I still kept trying.

The question remains, why did I stay somewhere I was clearly unwanted? Why did I try so hard for something that was a dead end street? I kept trying, kept pushing, kept hoping for a new road to be built, but instead there wasn't one and everything I was yearning for was out of reach.

I think the reason we stay holding on so long is because people like that know what they're doing. All it takes is one random compliment out of the blue, a nice gesture, something atypical of them and it sends us wanting more. It satisfies the feeling we felt all along because deep down we knew they were capable of being that person. The person they allowed us to see for a few seconds. We knew they weren't as cold as they present themselves.

It's that one second, that one compliment that keeps us hanging on. It makes us do crazy things, it makes us put in the 120 percent because more than anything we want them to love us. We want them to realize that they're lucky they have us and that we are better than they deserve, even though that will never make them want us more. It will never make them change. But we keep trying because we can't let them go.

9

Missing Someone Doesn't Mean They Belong In Your Life

I think about you damn near every day. I've been thinking about you since the day you entered my life.

You were, and still are, so tall and handsome with big, rough hands that drew me in. I wanted to know you, so I took my time and I learned who you were.

I learned how you slept and how you snored. I learned you weren't a breakfast person, but you loved your morning coffee. I learned you were kind, like really, genuinely kind. You cared about people and you wanted everyone to be included. I learned every time you sat on the couch you grabbed a pillow to wrap your arms around. I learned that you could only sleep in pitch black with the doors closed and you cringed over the fact that anyone could sleep with socks on.

And of everything I learned about you, the one thing I'm still certain of is that I still miss you terribly, but I know we don't belong in each other's lives.

I could call you, send you a text, show up at your door, do whatever I wanted to do to contact you, but that wouldn't change a thing. It wouldn't make us compatible because I'm admitting, yet again, that I miss you. Just because I miss you doesn't mean it would make everything work out.

All it would do is cause more pain. It would be like the cut that is almost healed being split wide open again.

I would love to crawl back into your bed one more time, I would love to kiss your lips and tell you how I've missed you, but it would be toxic.

It would be like I'm choosing to slowly kill myself.

I could love you again; I could call you and tell you I need you. But it would just rekindle the pain. It would be like breaking my leg again when it was in the process of healing. It would be like getting hit by a bus, then walking back out in traffic and getting hit again.

It would be like getting stabbed in the heart, then walking right back into the knife because I couldn't stay away.

As much as I miss you, I know we aren't meant for each other and we're definitely not good for each other.

You're the alcohol and I'm the painkillers, we're safe when we're alone, but together we're a dangerous combination.

I've been spending a lot of time trying to separate you from your memories. I've been trying to convince myself I miss the memories, not you. It's working a little, every day I try to think about you less. The pain of losing you is getting quieter.

I don't reach for you anymore in the morning and I don't sit around waiting for your call anymore at night.

I'm moving on and I'm trying to get stronger, but I still don't think there will ever come a day where I don't miss you, at least a little. But I'm getting there and I know going through the pain of missing you is just part of moving on.

You might forever live in my heart, but you'll no longer

live in my life. I'm moving on, for good this time. I'm done sabotaging my own heart going back to you because I can miss you all I want, but we will never be good for each other.

10

10 Signs You're Single AF (And Loving It)

1. You extremely value the relationships you do have.

Your relationships with your friends and family are super important to you because without them you wouldn't have anything. You can shower them with all the love you have in your heart and in turn they'll love you right back. It's awesome for you because you never have to compromise seeing them because you're free to do whatever fits your schedule and your schedule only!

2. You have a chocolate stash and a snack shelf (or shelves).

You keep whatever makes you happy in your kitchen and sometimes that's chocolate because who doesn't enjoy coming home after a long day and stuffing their face with a chocolate bar? Sometimes that's all you need to feel better. You don't have to worry about coming home and making dinner for someone; you can just kick back and eat from your snack shelf if that's all you feel like doing.

3. You love going out and not having a single worry (or staying in if that's more what you're feeling).

You'll be out tearing it up on the dance floor and having the time of your life because you have no worries or distractions. You can get drunk or have a casual couple beers; you can go home with someone or walk home by yourself. You can do whatever you're in the mood for because you don't have anyone to answer to. And if your weekend plans involve lounging out the couch in your PJs then go for it because you only have yourself to please!

4. You aren't constantly on your phone.

You can actually engage in conversation without looking at your phone. You don't have to keep staring at your phone waiting for a text back and you don't have to call to find out what someone else is doing constantly.

5. You say 'yes' to nearly everything.

If you get invited somewhere you're always the first person to say yes. You don't have to check in with anyone or sort out your plans. If you're free you go because adventure awaits.

6. You don't post #MCM pictures on Instagram and people LOVE you for it.

Seriously, how is that even a thing still? Everyone knows your

BF of 2 years is your #MCM. No one needs another reminder of that time you went on vacation together 6 months ago.

7. You always treat yo' self.

You don't have to pay for dinner for two or worry about starting a family (yet), you just get to worry about yourself and your needs. So if you want that ice cream, you get it. If you want that new dress, you go ahead and buy it. You do what you want because it's your money and all you're thinking about is you.

8. You learn to only rely on yourself and that's empowering.

If there is a spider in your one bedroom apartment, guess who's either killing it or sleeping with it in the corner of their ceiling? *You.* You have to do your own laundry, wash your own dishes, and do your own grocery shopping. You have to learn how to be self-sufficient on your own and it's actually pretty awesome to be like BOOM I did that shit on my own.

9. Your happiness doesn't depend on someone else.

If you're in a bad mood it's because something that happened in your life. You don't let what happened in someone else's day affect you. No one is coming home to you in a bad mood, and no one is taking their anger out on you. You create your own happiness by finding what makes you happy.

10. You can literally do whatever the hell you want with no worries.

And if nothing else on this list finds you at peace with being single, let this be the one. I literally moved out of my apartment, sold my belongings and moved across the world because that's what I wanted to do. Being single means you can actually do anything you want. Don't like where you live? Move. Want to travel? Hop on a plane. Want to quit the job you hate? Awesome, quit! Do whatever you want because at the end of the day the only person you have to please is yourself and that is wonderful.

11

When The Perpetually Single Girl Craves Love

She's prided herself for so long on being single, on being perfectly fine on her own, because she is. She's not single because no one wants her; she isn't unwanted or incapable of love. She just hasn't found someone to make her heart skip a beat. She hasn't found someone that fills her stomach with butterflies at the sight of them. She hasn't found someone she misses before they're even gone. She hasn't found someone to make her want to give up being single because her happiness was born in her decision to be single.

She loves being on her own; she has become her own saving grace and her own backbone. She's gone through loss, fights, hard times and good times without a S/O by her side. She's tough and she's been tough for others. She stands up for herself and makes sure she gets treated the way she deserves.

She doesn't need someone to complete her or fix her. She is whole on her own; she has filled her own voids, figured out how to fix things on her own. She can carry her own weight on her shoulders and she's proud of it.

She's found herself and she loves herself.

She's gotten used to being single, maybe a little to used to it.

She's become comfortable with it, maybe a little too comfortable with it.

There are times she gets lonely because life isn't meant to be lived alone all the time. Even though she can do things for herself, on her own, doesn't necessarily means she always wants to.

There are times when—even though she can carry all her groceries inside in two loads—sometimes she'd rather have someone there to help her do it in one. There are times that instead of putting air in her own tires sometimes she'd like someone to do it for her. There are times that she would rather share the grill with someone instead of always grilling her own burgers.

There are times that instead of coming home to an empty house and cooking dinner for herself she would rather be cooking dinner for someone else. There are times that she would rather be waking up to someone she loves instead of waking up alone. There are times she would rather cook breakfast for two, make coffee for two and have someone to share her mornings with.

Because as strong, as independent, as happy as she is on her own sometimes she just needs a hand to hold. Someone to kiss her when she's feeling down, someone to tell her she looks beautiful when she's doubting herself, someone to be goofy when she's upset because as great as being single is, it isn't better than love.

Even the perpetually single girl craves love, craves attention and craves the feeling of being wanted. As much as she craves it, it isn't that easy to find. There have been guys who have come and gone, guys who haven't stuck around, and guys who broke her heart, so she started being guarded. She started choosing herself, she started putting herself first and before she realized it she started becoming happier that way.

She started finding happiness in herself, she stopped getting let down, she stopped getting her heart broken. She became strong and it led her to where she is now, but even the perpetually single girl craves love because it's a long trip alone.

12

Sleeping With Him Won't Make Him Like You (At Least Not For Long)

I've been there, thinking maybe, just maybe, if I hooked up with him he would like me more. I told myself it would make me more desirable. I thought maybe if we hook up his feelings would change for some inexplicable reason.

But they won't. And I already knew that.

The first time I had sex, I made the guy I was talking to wait seven months. But after seven months he still didn't love me, let alone like me enough to label our relationship. I thought having sex with him would make me feel better about our relationship, and it didn't. I thought having sex with him would make him want to take our relationship to the next level, and it didn't.

The only thing he liked more about me was now he could have sex with me.

Sleeping with him won't change his mind about anything. Sleeping with him won't make him realize he can't live his life without you. Sleeping with him won't make him want to wake up next to you every morning for the rest of his life. Sleeping with him won't make you want to do any of those things. Sleeping with him won't make him stay.

You've got to stop hoping it can become something more, stop hoping that sex will change him, and stop banking that there could be future potential because the reality of it is if he wanted future potential he would make it known.

By sleeping with him you really just gave him all he wanted. He had you; he got what he wanted and now really has no other reason to stay hanging around. **He has nothing more to imagine or curiosity lingering around in his mind about you.** He got what he wanted because you hoped it would make him stay.

He might have seemed so genuine and interested, he might have said convincing words, and he might have told you empty promises to feel like he's gained your trust. You really wanted him; you wanted to feel desired by him, so you gave in and he got what he ultimately wanted.

If he really wanted to know you, to make plans with you, he wouldn't have tried to get to know you in bed.

He would have wanted to know who you are as a person. He would have wanted to know where you come from and what makes you smile from ear to ear. He would have wanted to know what your guilty pleasures are and how much food you can eat. He would have wanted to know the more meaningful stuff, the things you can only learn by spending time with someone.

Sleeping with him won't make him want to learn about you. You could be everything he has ever wanted in a girl, but if he isn't interested in a relationship it doesn't matter who you are. He's made up his mind.

Don't sleep with him because he bought you something.

Don't sleep with him because you feel guilty. Don't sleep with him because you feel you have something to prove. Don't sleep with him because you want him to like you because it won't work.

Men will do crazy things to get a woman to sleep with him, don't fall into the trap, don't be the one who thinks you can change him, because you can't. Sleeping with him won't make him stay, so please, only do it if you're ready because either way you're giving him everything he wants. And sleeping with him won't make him like you, especially not after your clothes are back on.

13

Don't Date The Guy Who Refuses To Talk About What You Are

I've been there, wasting so much precious time just 'talking' to the guy who I opened up my heart to completely. I've spent hours thinking in my head whether or not I should ask the ever so dreaded question of "what are we" because that question tends to send people running as fast and far away as they can go.

It was my freshman year of college up until the very beginning of my junior year with lots of mixed signals and confusion. I'd ask the question, "Where is this going?" but the answer would never change much.

"I don't know, we're just having fun," or "I'm not sure, let's just keep doing our thing."

What the hell is our thing?! Do you want to date me or not?

It was basically any variation of "I don't have the answer you want so I'm going to avoid the question and try to be nice about it."

Ladies, we've all been there. Lingering around being there when it is convenient for him. We do stupid things; we wait up late at night in hopes for a text, hoping he will say, "Come over." We hope he shows us some vulnerability and lets us in. We hope we can finally stop 'talking' and start dating.

But we need to stop.

Why do we want to date the guy who refuses to talk about what we are? Why do we keep seeking those types of guys out over and over? Constantly getting let down.

The main thing a relationship needs is communication and that is what has been lacking since the very beginning.

We don't know when it's too early to bring up the question because you've probably already been 'talking' for a few months. You want this relationship to progress but you just can't figure out what is going on inside his head because he keeps giving you mixed signals.

Some days he seems really into it and everything seems perfect. You're convinced he likes you and you spent the best day together. Then he gets flaky again. You wonder where you went wrong. You question if he likes you, and you drive yourself crazy trying to dissect every little thing. But you only think those thoughts in your head or say them out loud to your friends, asking for advice from them because no matter what you can't ask him what's going on.

If you ask me it's SO stupid and I can say that because I have been that girl too.

If he won't talk to you about his feelings or what he wants out of whatever you are then he's really not interested in you. You can fill a journal with excuses of why he is different, you can defend him and tell yourself he isn't a bad guy and he makes you happy. But the reality is if you're asking then he isn't giving you what you want.

Remember the guy who used to blow up your phone? He'd

consistently be asking you to do things, to go out, even if you said no the first five times. But to you he was too easy; you didn't want him because there was no chase, and we all love the chase. It builds desire and intimacy. You could have had that guy, because he actually liked you, he wanted you, he was interested and made it a point to be known by repeatedly making an effort even if he got rejected the first few times around.

But the guy who won't talk to you about what you are is not interested. I hate to break it to you. I wish I could put some nice spin on it, but I can't because the truth is if he is interested in you he will make it known. He will do dumb things, he will embarrass himself and he will make his presence known. Just like you are doing to the guy who won't talk to you about what you are.

Move on, walk away, and let him go. It might be months or years of hanging on but it's time to finally let go and walk away. It's time to be alone and embrace being single. Truly single. Stop looking at your phone waiting for a text, stop obsessively checking his favorites. It's time to cut the rope you've been hanging on to and feel what it's like to live for yourself again.

Walking away from the wrong guy will open up your heart to finding the right guy because he is out there and you will be good enough for him. He will love you and most of all, he will communicate with you about what you are.

14

Maybe In Another Life Our Hearts Would Intertwine

Maybe in another life our paths wouldn't have just crossed, but intertwined. Maybe I would have been able to love you the way you loved me.

Maybe there is a life where I want what you want.

Maybe there is a life where I want to graduate college with you and move back to your hometown. Maybe I'd want to start a family with you and buy a house. Maybe I'd love to decorate a baby's room with you, with wallpaper and cute little décor everywhere. Maybe you'd be the one to make me want to settle down and set a foundation for my life.

But it's not in this life.

In this life I don't want to settle down, I don't want to stay in one place, I don't want a relationship yet, and I surely don't want a family.

Maybe in another life you would be everything I hope for, everything I dream about at night when I'm lonely. Maybe you'd be the one I'd love to come home to after having the worst day imaginable. Maybe you'd be the one I'd crawl into bed with and never let go of. Maybe you'd be the one whose shoulder I'd be burying my face into when a scary movie is on.

Maybe in another life you'd be the one I'd be planning family vacations with, instead of just planning solo trips for me. Maybe in another life I would want that, to go with a family, my own family. Maybe I'd love to pack my kids a suitcase and help situate them in their car seats. Maybe I'd enjoy seeing their faces as we board an airplane and maybe I'd love taking pictures with them at Disney.

But I've never been a kid person and those plans don't fit into my five or ten year plan. As much as you care about me and as many nice things you do for me, I just can't love you back.

Maybe in another life I wouldn't be so unsure of everything. Maybe I wouldn't spend so much time overthinking and wondering what my life could be like if I traveled here or moved there. Maybe if I knew what I wanted I could settle down, but I don't, not in this life anyway.

This lifetime wasn't meant for us to be together. Our stars didn't properly align and I know it might break your heart, but you wouldn't want to be with someone like me anyway. Someone so reckless and indecisive. Someone who constantly pushes others away. Someone who blacks out reality and doesn't allow herself to miss others because it's easier that way.

You don't want someone like me, you deserve someone who will love you forever and grow old with you.

And maybe there is a life where we grow old together, sitting on the front porch swinging back and forth. Maybe there is a life where we have spent a lifetime together, raising a family, pouring each other morning coffee and kissing each other goodnight.

If there is one thing I'm certain of in this life it's that I will always break your heart. I will never be able to intertwine my heart with yours. As much as I wish I could sometimes, I know it's better off this way.

You will find someone who loves you the way you love her. Maybe when that happens I will feel regret, because my heart breaks every time I know we won't end up together. But that is something I will have to live with.

Maybe in another life needing you would be the only thing that's on my mind, but in this life I just can't love you back.

15

You Get To Write Your Own Love Story

No two stories are the same.

Maybe you had an instant connection; he had you from "hello." Maybe it took longer. Maybe it took him asking you five times to go on a date before you said yes. Maybe your love started as a friendship and developed into something more. Maybe you started off as friends with benefits but it turned into love.

The possibilities are endless because everyone has their own story.

Don't base your expectation off of your friend's relationship; don't set unrealistic standards in your head of how you want things to work out. Don't draw out the perfect man in your head and be disappointed in everyone who comes your way that doesn't meet those specific requirements. Often times that person doesn't exist and while your busy searching for the perfect guy the right guy could be right in front of you.

Open your heart to love. Love every person you come across. You can love anyone you want because love has no rules. Your heart wants what your heart wants, as cliché as it is; it's also something beautiful. Love can blossom out of the most simplistic or strangest relationships because you don't get to choose who you love, but you get to choose how you love them.

You get to decide how you want to romance each other, entertain each other and how you live your life together. You can choose where to live, how to live, what to do with your lives.

You can sell everything you own and travel the world. You can buy a camper and constantly move around from place to place. You can spend your years backpacking and exploring everything the world has to offer together. You can go on adventure after adventure and spend your life making memories and not spend money on a home because to you maybe that isn't important.

You can settle down together and put down roots. You can save your money and buy a home together, or build one. You can live in a big home in the country or live in a little city apartment building. You can settle down wherever and however you want. You can decide to start a family or focus on your careers. You can get a dog, or six, and spend your free time walking them and loving them.

The possibilities of your life together are endless because you can write your own love story. You can choose how you want to live. How you want to experience life. You can discover your own happiness.

Don't listen to others tell you what to do, don't listen to anyone tell you how to live out your love story. If you don't want to get married, don't. If you know you've found the perfect person you can't live without them get married, move in with them as fast or as slow as you want!

Don't miss out on an opportunity to have and feel true love

because to find someone you wake up next to every day and truly love with every fiber in you is rare, but it's possible.

Find your person and live out your fairytale. Do whatever makes you happy because in the end when the outside noises and factors fade all you will have is each other.

16

In A Room Full Of Everyone I've Ever Loved, I'd Still Choose You

I used to be the girl that made you laugh and the girl that got to spend all night watching movies with you on the couch. I used to be the girl that would always be riding shotgun next to you singing at the top our of lungs. I used to be the girl you'd call when you wanted to go on an adventure and I'd go anywhere with you.

I used to be the girl who could finish your sentences and think of the words when you couldn't. I used to be the girl who was constantly on your mind, dawn till dusk and then dusk till dawn. I used to be the girl who would leave you wide-awake all night talking and thinking.

I used to be the girl who was your everything before I became the girl who was your nothing.

I stopped being the first girl you wanted to talk to in the morning. I stopped being the one you couldn't wait to see after work. I stopped being the one you'd take out to dinner. I stopped being the one you wanted to spend your time with.

You broke me. You made me feel like my heart was ripped out of my chest and stomped on a million times. I felt pain over and over; when I thought it started going away it came back. It always came back.

But if you put me in a room full of everyone I've ever loved and everyone who has ever broken my heart, I'd still choose you. I would always choose you.

I would run to you over and over again. Every time. I would wrap my arms around you and tell you how I've missed you every day since you've been gone.

It's you I would choose you to wake up next to every morning and make breakfast for. It's you I would choose to send flirty texts to on my lunch break. It's you I would choose you to come home to after a long, shitty day because I know just the site of you would make me feel better.

I would choose you no matter how much alcohol I had in my system, even in a room full of everyone I've ever loved because to me we had something that was rare and intense. An instant connection I knew I never wanted to live without, but you must not have felt the same after time. As I grew with you, you grew away.

Even so, I would choose you when I'm lonely and want someone by my side, but I would also choose you when it's 2 PM and something wonderful has happened. You'd be the person I'd want by my side when all my dreams come true.

Because it's not about who you miss when it's the middle of the night and you're lonely, it's about who you miss in the middle of the day when you've got a million things going on. And to me that person is always you.

No matter the circumstances, no matter the time, if I had to choose again I would always choose you, even if you wouldn't choose me too.

17

If He Tries To Change You, Please Don't Date Him

Don't date the guy who thinks he is better than everyone else because he will always be that way and that isn't someone you want to be associated with.

Don't date the guy who thinks that he can come through and tear up everything in his path without any repercussions because he will soon enough tear through every relationship he built.

Don't date the guy who constantly acts like he doesn't give a damn about anything, because in reality he probably won't give a damn about you either.

Don't date the guy who is a player because no matter how hard you try and how hard you want to change him, you can't.

Don't date the guy who acts uninterested. Who keeps you hanging around, who only gives you an indication every now and then that he is interested in you because to him you will always just be an after thought. He will only end up breaking your heart.

Don't date the guy who only texts you at 2:30 AM. Even though you might desire him and wait up for his text message, he won't be loyal. He only wants you when he's horny or lonely and you deserve more than that.

Above all else, don't date the guy who wants to change you.

Don't date the guy who buys you fancy items because he wants you too look and dress a certain way. Don't date the guy who tells you to put on make up before you leave the house because he is embarrassed to be seen with you otherwise. Don't date the guy who tries you change you into his form of "perfect" whatever that is.

Don't date someone who doesn't love you for you because he is holding you back from being with someone who will truly love the way you laugh and the way you cry. He will be happy to be by you on your worst days, as well as your best. He will love you for you because you are incredible just the way you are and no one should try to make you feel like you're not amazing.

Don't date the guy who makes you feel like you aren't good enough, that you're not deserving of love, that you're not smart, or that you're not independent. Don't date someone who tries to hold you back from your true potential because he is scared you will realize just how great you are.

Don't date someone who tries to belittle you and makes you feel guilty for the things you like and you want to do. Don't date someone who tells you what to say and what not to say, what to post and what not to post. Don't date someone who tells you who you can and cannot talk to.

Don't date someone who tries to restrict you from your life.

Don't date someone who tries to control you in any aspect of life. You are human and you are allowed to make your own decision and be your own person. You are allowed to do what makes you happy. You are allowed to laugh and cry and have bad days. You are allowed to eat what you want and dress how you please. You are allowed everything and anything because the world is at your fingertips and no one should be trying to take that from you.

Whatever you do, please do not date someone who tries to change you because you are already great the way you are and you can't fix something that isn't broken.

18

As Your Life Goes On, Please Remember Me

I want you to remember me as the first girl who loved you and the first girl you loved back. I want you to remember our first kiss in the car when you dropped me off at home by my front door. I want you to remember the first time you told me you'd miss me when I was going away on vacation.

I want you to think of me when it's windy and how we used to race to the car. I want you to remember how you used to grab me, spin me around, and push my hair out of my face before you'd kiss me.

I want you to remember me by every place that became "ours" because "our spots" became our happy places. I want you to drive by and think of me like I think of you.

I want you to remember me when you start getting overwhelmed, even if you refuse to admit that you're stressed out. I want you to think of my voice telling you everything is going to be just fine. I want you to breathe in and out like I'm right there with you, and I want you to think in your head that breathing doesn't help anything because I know in your stubborn head that's what you're thinking.

I want you to remember how smart you are, no matter how many rejection letters you may receive. I want you to remember that you are capable of doing anything you want to and that you will succeed as long as you have the passion and heart to do it.

I want you to remember me when it's Christmastime and there are lights lining the streets and the malls. I want you to think of me when you find the perfect gift and I want you to be excited to wrap it, even though I won't be by your side to help you fix it.

I want you to remember me when you're out walking, wherever it may be. By the river as you cast your reel, through the woods as you walk your dog, through the city as you're out exploring. I want you to remember how we talked and laughed when we were alone in silence of the world. I want you to remember how comfortable we were with each other and how I always kept your trust.

I want you to remember how you used to wrap your arms around me and tell me there was no other place you'd rather be than here. I want you to remember how you used to wipe the tears right off my face and tell me everything was going to be okay.

I want you to remember me as kind, and loving, and passionate. I want you to remember me as caring, and strong, and supportive. I want you to remember me as the girl who was once your everything.

I want you to look back on our time together and know that what we had was wonderful. I want you to remember our love when you're out in the world pursuing this brave new world you're seeking and I'll remember you when I'm making a home in mine because part of you will always live in me.

I want you to remember everything about our relationship

because I want you to treat the next girl just as good, if not better. You gave me the world, even though our worlds didn't align. As strong as our love ever was, you'll find better love.

19

I Only Want Forever Relationships

I'm a forever kind of person because if I'm going to invest in something I want to wholly invest in it. I'm not a half ass two things kind of person; I'm a whole ass one-thing kind of person, because if you don't put your whole heart into something then there is no point in pursuing it.

I don't want mediocre relationships that will fizzle and fade. I want realistic relationships that will last forever, not even only pertaining to love, but with friendships and relationships in general.

I want to be surrounded by people who make my heart pound and skip a beat because their presence makes me so happy. I want to be around people who inspire me and make me want to be better and do better. I want to be around people who I know will be there for me forever through the thick and thin because I will absolutely be that person for them. I want to be surrounded by people who actually want to be around me and don't leave me wondering where I stand with them.

I want to be the old couple one day sitting on my front porch swing looking at the man next to me knowing this is my forever and knowing that I wouldn't have wanted it any other way. I want to fall in love with him over and over until we're old and gray. But I don't want to stop doing things for each other, even when we're 80 I still want to love like we're 30.

I want to be head over heels, and I know it's possible because I've seen it. I've seen a man order his wife's favorite food even after she's passed because he couldn't stand eating alone and her meal made him remember her. I've driven past the couple who spent every single summer day in their yard swing together rocking back and forth talking about life. I've seen old men still carry their wife's tray and pay for her meals.

I know that forever kind of love exists and I want it.

I want to be old and gray and still talk to my friends from childhood or college. Even though we won't be as young and reckless as we once were I still want to reminisce over the good times. I want to laugh at the hungover kids that walk in our favorite coffee shop on the weekends talking about all they did the night before like we've all done so many times.

I don't invest in relationships I know won't last because to me there is no point. When I want something I want it for good and I want it forever. Maybe that's why I'm still on my own in terms of my love life.

I've had people come and go, but no one I could really see a future with, and to me that isn't worth the investment. I don't want to wind up getting my heart broken if I know it isn't going to last, if I know he won't be rocking beside me in the future.

I want people in my life that make forever seem too short. I only want forever relationships because when I'm old and gray, I want the people by my side who have been there for everything. That is when it matters most.

20

Today I'm Finally Letting You Go

Today I'm done holding on to your memory. I'm throwing away all the cards and love letters I've held on to for far too long. I'm ripping up every picture I have stashed away in my drawer to remember us. I'm giving your old shirts away to someone who doesn't know their significance.

I'm letting you go, completely.

I don't want to scroll through my camera roll and see old pictures of you. I don't want to be searching through my contacts and see your name come up anymore. I don't want to find old screen shots of our conversations. I don't want to hear old songs and think of you.

It's not that I want to forget about you, because I don't, not completely anyway. You became a huge part of my life, but that's the thing. You were just a part of it.

It's about moving on, I have to move on. It's about me not thinking about you every time something good happens and wanting to run to you with the news. It's about being able to handle all the bad on my own. It's about me picking up my life and moving on without wondering what you're doing with yours.

It's letting go of the idea I thought I would spend the rest of my life with you. It's leaving behind the traces of you that you imprinted everywhere. It's being okay with being on my own.

It's about running into you and not having my heart skip a beat, it's about not getting tongue tied and nervous about what you're thinking about me. It's actually not caring anymore about what you do think of me. I don't want to get butterflies when you say my name. I don't want to be tossing and turning over the thoughts of missing you.

I'm letting you go because I want to be happy. I want to be able to be happy for you, too. I want to be okay with the fact someone else gets to spend forever with you. I want to be okay with the fact I won't be waking up next to you again, and that someone else will be pouring your coffee with two creams and two sugars. I want to be okay with the fact someone else is loving your tattoos and your rough hands.

I want to be healed and I want to be whole so that I can find happiness with someone new.

So today I'm finally letting you go because you and I are no longer anything and holding on to you is only hurting me. Today I decided I need to put myself first and leave you behind for good.

21

You Might Not Be Enough For Him, But You're Enough For Someone Else

He's the one that keeps you up at night, rolling around in your bed, clinging to your pillow wishing it were him. He's the one you get all knock-kneed and make a fool of yourself in front of because you just want him to like you or even notice you the way you notice him. He's the one you go out of your way for and spend extra long perfecting your hair for, even though you're not sure if he even notices.

The harsh truth is, he might never notice. He might never think of you at night, even when he's feeling lonely. He might not think twice about your kind gestures and he might think your goofy, awkward laugh isn't cute.

But who cares?

The guy you have to basically throw yourself at isn't the kind of guy you want to be with. You don't want to have to fight for his attention; you don't want to have to make a fool of yourself for someone to notice you because while you're noticing him he might be noticing someone else.

You don't want to be someone's second choice, if you're

even that. You deserve more than that. You deserve someone to love you unconditionally, someone to put you first and someone to be standing in your corner no matter what.

To him you might not be tall enough, or maybe you're too tall. You might be too thick or too skinny; you might not have the right hair color or be 'too pale.' The thing is, though, someone else will love all those things about you, they will love you for who you are. Every little flaw you find in yourself they will love and cherish.

Because really, you don't want to be with someone you have to convince to love you because you can't force love.

Even if that guy doesn't love you, someone else will because you will find the other half of your soul. Someone will love you for you, they will love you for all the weird, quirky things you do when you don't think anyone is watching. They will love you for those things because they think it's adorable and cute. They will love you for being wholly and unapologetically you.

They will love you when you when you're sick and miserable because they care about every part of you. They will love you when you're crying over your favorite show because something heart breaking happened. They will love you when you've just achieved your dream job because they are so proud of you.

They will want to be by your side the entire time because no matter what, you are enough for them.

You will no longer linger in the maybe section, you will no longer wonder if the guy on your mind is also thinking of you because he won't make you wonder. You will become his everything, he will put you first and he will make it known.

When the right guy comes around you won't have to wonder if you matter because you will know. You will be someone's everything and you will be enough for them, just the way you are.

22

When You Can't Help Missing Him (But You Hate Yourself For It)

He was your kryptonite, your weakness, and your biggest downfall. You knew he wasn't good for you but you still couldn't resist him, no matter how hard you tried. He became your realm and he had you from hello.

Part of you knew this would happen. You knew you should have stayed away from him, you told yourself that, but your head and your heart wanted two different things. How cliché, right?

When he was around the sun burned brighter and the world turned faster; he became the center of your tiny world and made it feel so much bigger. He didn't have to do much, but the feelings he gave you were immense, and as hard you tried, you couldn't push them away.

And even now that things are over, you still lie in bed at night thinking of him. You think of all the way he destroyed you and smashed your perfectly good heart into millions of tiny pieces. It kills you, but you know deep inside if you could redo it, start again, choose to love him or not, you'd do it all over.

You hate yourself for loving him, because you shouldn't.

He's moved on while you're still mulling over the thought of him; he has become your muse and no matter how hard you try you can't get him out of your head.

You hate that you would love him all over again. You would dive back into his arms and let him scoop you up. You would pick up where you left off because you hate that you can't make it through a single day without thinking of him, without wondering if he's wondering about you, even though you know the answer.

Even if you say a hundred times a day that you hate him, the truth is that you don't hate him for not loving you anymore, but you hate yourself for still loving him.

Loving him was like being found when you've been lost for so long. He made you feel safe and loved. He made you feel cared about and not overlooked. He made you feel appreciated by all the words he said. But words are just words and eventually his actions stopped meeting the appealing lines that soared out of his mouth. Other things, new things, started filling his pretty little head and those things soon found a more important place with him.

You just wish you could call him and tell him how stupid he is and how much you miss him, but you knew it wouldn't change a thing. You'd stand on a rooftop and scream it if you could because maybe it would make you feel better even though he's gone part of him still lives inside you, a part you hate, but at the same time don't want to let go of.

But you need to let go.

He just comes back in flashes, so bright and so forceful. It makes it hard to live without him.

He's like a kaleidoscope of memories that just flash in front of your eyes. He fills your head with thoughts that you can't forget.

He's like the devil pulling you in with such a handsome smile that you can't resist.

You pretend not to care; you say no when people ask if you miss him. You try to convince yourself you're over him and that you don't want to run into him. You pretend your stomach doesn't sink when his name is brought up and you pretend you don't love him when the whole world knows you do.

As much as you tell yourself one day he will miss you, deep down you know it probably isn't true, so you just wait for the day where you stop missing him, too.

23

Wanting True Love Does Not Make You Weak

I've always prided myself on being single, on not needing anyone to make me happy because I'm already pretty damn happy with my life on my own. I've always thought of myself as a strong person, I always thought I had to be the role model for all my single friends reminding them that being single is incredible and to be strong as well. And while that is still true, **I'm coming to the point where I do want love and I do want to find someone to spend my time with.**

Admitting to wanting love usually comes hand in hand with being called desperate or needy. We shame people for admitting to what we all virtually want, which is love. It makes us feel vulnerable and exposed to come out and say we want it. It's like your opening your heart and mind to an idea you've tried to close off for so long.

Wanting love is not bad, it is not wrong, and it certainly does not make you weak.

Everyone tells you that your twenties are your selfish years; those words have come out of my mouth as well. I graduated college, left everyone behind, and moved to the other side of the world on a one-way ticket. I can't tell a single person when

I'm coming back home or what my timeline is because I have no idea.

I also realize I'm only 22 and I'm still young. People tell me to focus on my career and get my goals in line, which I am doing. I know what I want to do and I strongly believe I'm on the right path. I did put my own dreams first; I moved to adventure, explore, and begin my life of traveling that I've always wanted so desperately to live.

No one can tell me I'm not out living my dreams. No one can tell me I'm not prioritizing my goals and career objectives because I am.

The only thing I don't understand is why can't I want a relationship in the mix of all this?

I want someone to join me on my adventures. I want someone by my side that wants to go to New Zealand and go sky-diving. I want someone who would love to spend a weekend scuba diving or snorkeling the Great Barrier Reef. I would love to have someone who is all for living out of backpacks and volunteering at sanctuaries along the way. **That fits into my dreams, and that goes with my plan.**

I'm not aiming to find my husband and get married by 25. I don't need that. I don't need a house and a family right away. I still want to be able to live out my adventures and dreams, but just because I want to do that doesn't mean I have to do it alone.

I just need the right person to come along, the other adventurous soul that wants to join me on my journey because my journey is also in fact his journey.

Wanting love is never bad, it is never something you should be shamed for because wanting love is natural and it's instinct.

Never let someone make you feel ashamed for wanting love, because wanting to go on dates and spend time with someone you have interest in is never a waste of time.

Everyone has their own idea of love; they have their own ideal fairy tale in their head or maybe it isn't a fairy tale. Maybe they just want someone who loves them back and makes them happy. Maybe they don't need a big adventure or a diamond ring; they are perfectly happy just with someone by their side through it all.

I love the idea of being in love. I love the idea of finding someone that just feels like home, like the piece of you that's always been missing.

I've always admired my friends' and coworkers' relationships. I've always been looking forward to that one day where I have my own someone to love.

As much as I do understand the importance of putting yourself first along with your goals and dreams, I *don't* understand why people frown so much when throwing a relationship into that mix. A relationship needs nurturing and attention just like every other aspect of your life.

Wanting love makes you strong, because even in this crazy modern day dating world we live in, you still believe in love.

You haven't given up, you haven't decided to quit when you've met another person who has no intentions of staying. You shake it off and don't let it shatter your heart. You keep believing.

I know I am young and my time will come, but I know I'm not the only one who feels this way. Wanting love is not a bad thing, it is not something you should feel shameful or embarrassed for wanting, it's a good thing. It means you still have hope for what's to come, and when it comes it will be worth the wait.

24

I'm A 'Love You Forever' Not 'Just For One Night' Kind Of Girl

I'm not a "go home with someone you just met while drunk at a bar" type of girl. I'm not a "hook up and leave at 4 AM" kind of girl. I'm not a "text and show up for sex" kind of girl. **And I'm definitely not a one-night stand type of girl.**

I've never planned my outfit to look 'hot enough' to bring someone home. I've never done my makeup in hopes that someone finds my eyes intriguing and daring. I've never planned on going out and finding someone to come home with.

I've never been able to free myself from my mind and my fears to find someone at a hole in the wall kind of bar or night-club and felt comfortable enough to take them home, and I don't think I ever will be.

I'll never be able to let down my hair and fall on a strangers bed. I'll never be able to sleep with someone whose first name I might not remember. I'll never be able to get naked for someone I don't have any connection with.

It's just not me and it never will be, and that's okay.

I know myself well enough to know that a one-night stand

would leave me empty and full of regret. It would leave me feeling ashamed of myself and that isn't worth it to me.

There is nothing wrong with one-night stands; there is nothing wrong with getting dressed up and going out with the intention of not coming home alone. There is nothing wrong with not knowing his first name, because maybe it's easier that way, but I've never been one for awkward goodbyes and meaningless sex because I'm the girl who needs something more.

I'm the girl that wants love. I want to fall into the same bed a million times and feel completely comfortable and at home with whoever I decide to settle down with.

I want to go out with him and come home with him. I want to come home and make weird concoctions of drunk food from what we can find in our fridge.

I want to laugh and make a mess; I want to forget about it until the morning because I want to rush off to bed with him. I want to love each other like it's the first time we've ever been in love; carefree and full of love to give each other. I want to go home with someone who I know cares about me and wants to love me for who I am, not how I looked in a dark, hazy bar.

I want to wake up next to him, in his arms, I want to kiss him good morning and know that I will get to do that for the rest our of lives together.

I want to find comfort in him and a happiness I wouldn't find in the arms of a stranger. I want him to feel like home.

I want to run to the kitchen and make breakfast for two because I don't just want someone to be there in the morning, I want more than that. I want someone who makes breakfast with me, every single morning. I want to laugh at the mess we made the night before and the only thing I want to regret is how much junk food we ate.

I have never been and never will be a one-night stand kind of girl because I want more than that. I've always wanted more than that.

I'm an all or nothing kind of person.

If I want something I dive in fully, I don't just dip my toes in. I want more than meaningless sex because I know more is out there and in the mean time I'd rather be alone than with someone who doesn't know what makes me laugh and what cheers me up when I'm down.

I'm not a one-night stand type of girl, I'm not into Netflix and chill, I'm not the one you can call up late at night when you're lonely because **I've always wanted more.** I've always wanted to mean something more and I'm proud of that.

25

I Want The Kind Of Love Our Grandparents Had

I want an old-fashioned love where we take things slow, where we don't dive right in and move at lightning speed. I want to go on dates; I want to figure out the person from what they tell me and what their behaviors show me, not by what they post on Instagram.

I want someone to ask me out on a date, a real date, not a "let's hang out" date. I want to spend hours getting ready and dance around my room with my friends. I want to have him pick me up at a certain time and have butterflies in my stomach as I walk to his car.

I want to sit down at a restaurant and have an actual, meaningful conversation. I don't want to gossip or talk about the latest trends, I want to talk about life and our backgrounds. I want to listen to the words he has to say as he sits across from me and I want him to do the same for me. I don't want to be competing with a phone for attention.

I want to take a walk afterwards because it goes so well. I want to walk along the streetlights, laughing and feeling hopeful thoughts in my head. I want him to drive me home after and walk me to the front door. I want to feel that sense of nerves wondering and hoping he will kiss me before he leaves, with no expectations of staying the night or hooking up.

But more than any of that, I want him to mean what he says when he brings me home. I want him to be honest if he had fun and I want him to mean it if he plans to talk to me soon.

I don't want to wait around for days on end, hoping he might text me or Tweet something about me. I want him to call me; I want to hear his voice. I don't want the games, I don't want the rules, I want honesty and I want him to be upfront.

And if it does go well and I do hear from him again, I want an old fashioned kind of love. I want him to walk to my house with flowers and surprise me just because, I want him to hold the door for me because it's the proper thing to do. I don't need loads of gifts, I don't need a "In A Relationship" post on Facebook, all I want is someone who is upfront and honest. Someone who doesn't make me question if they love me and if they want me around.

I want someone to bring me a care package just because I don't feel well. I want someone to plan surprise trips for us to go on. I want someone to do romantic things for me because those little things are what is important.

I want someone who will fight for us when things get rough and not just bolt at the first sign of hardship. I want someone who will talk through our problems and not let their frustration get the best of them. I want someone who won't just get up and walk out the door because problems are inevitable, but there is always a way to work to the solution.

And of all the wants I have, I also have a ton of love I want to give.

I want to make him coffee in the morning and cook breakfast for him. I want to surprise him with little romantic gestures as much as I want to be surprised. I want to take care of him when he's sick. I want to write him notes and call him when he's away. I want to do just as much for him, if not more, than he does for me.

I want someone who wants to love like our grandparents did, because if I learned anything from them it's that they got it right.

26

Love When You're Ready, Not When You're Lonely

I've been in love once, my first and only love. When I was with him my world felt better, at least for a portion of our relationship. Then I noticed the direction we were going had changed. His plans didn't match mine, especially for how young we were. He started becoming controlling (or maybe I just finally realized he was controlling) and as much as it hurt me I had to let go.

After the tears had slowed down I started finding myself going for guys I had no business going for.

I started looking for love because I didn't want to be alone.

I would stay at my guy friends' houses so that I didn't have to sleep alone. I would look for and force connections that weren't really there, and I'd spend so much time convincing myself I was happy when I truly wasn't.

I tried to tell my head and heart I didn't miss my ex; I tried to tell myself things were better. That way as I prayed no one would hear me crying in the shower because I wanted to be strong.

I wanted to seem together because I didn't want months to

go by and have people think I was weak, or pathetic, or tell me to move on.

But what I didn't know then is you can't put a broken heart back together in a certain amount of time. You're allowed to feel the pain and sadness for as long as you need.

Heartbreak doesn't have an expiration date; you don't wake up one morning and suddenly forget the way he made you feel.

Learning to live without someone you started building your life around isn't easy to get over. I didn't know what to do with my feelings. I tried being so strong on the outside while feeling so weak on the inside. I was convinced breaking up with him was a mistake, but he moved on so quickly while I was still trying to find the shattered pieces of my heart.

Then the loneliness set in. Feeling alone makes you think irrational thoughts. You start falling in lust with every person you show interest in or every person who shows interest in you.

There is no stability or sign of commitment, but there's a fire burning and the flame is what's keeping you warm now.

Lust is sloppy and it's needy; you don't have a real emotional connection, but you feel like you need them. You want to know what they're doing and if they're thinking of you. Without their attention you feel like your world is falling apart because you crave the attention so much.

You should be alone after you break up. You should be alone for as much time as you need to heal, because eventually the pain of your heart break won't be screaming in your ear as much as it used to about how much you miss your ex.

There are some people who will never get over someone

they love, and that's okay, too. But before you start a new relationship you should be ready. You should have come to terms with being alone and figured out who you are as a person now. You should have figured out what makes you happy and what you want or don't want in a future partner.

A love bred out of loneliness is not a love you want to be in.

You should date someone who you could happily see a forever with because really, what's the point of dating someone if you don't see marriage in the future? Or at least think you could down the line?

Know your worth. Know when you're ready to submerge yourself into a new love. **Don't dive in if you can't fully commit.** You should love when you're ready to fall in love a million times with the same person. You should love when you're ready to fall in love with the same person every day. You should love when the sight of them makes your bad day better. You should love when the sound of their laugh makes you laugh, and you should love when you get to wake up every morning and they're by your side.

Be secure in who you are on your own because being alone is important. It helps you find your strength and learn who you are, it makes you realize it's better to be alone than with someone who isn't fully invested. So please, don't allow your loneliness to fool you into the arms of someone who you know you have no business being with. **Be alone**, you'll be surprised how much it can teach you.

27

I Want The Kind Of Love That Makes Me A Better Person

I long for the love that is written about in novels with the pain, heartache, and happy ending. A love that is built on hardships and overcoming triumphs together. A love that is beautiful and real. A love that is passionate and honest, not a love that is easy and comfortable.

I don't want perfect love, but I want a motivational love. A love that is founded on desire and hope; a love that makes me certain that together we can truly do anything. I don't want love that is only great at the beginning but continues to be great and growing until the end.

I want the kind of love that makes me want to be a better person.

A love that is filled with passion and erases some of the self-doubt I have in my mind. I want a love that inspires me to wake up before the sun and go to the gym. I want a love that inspires me to eat healthy to better myself. I want a love that has me swimming in novels, reading all the best lines combined into a masterpiece. I want a love that makes me feel alive and peaceful, not drained and worthless. **I want a**

love that inspires me to be kinder and more generous to the world around me just by looking at the person by my side.

I want someone who will make me feel more alive. Someone who will push me out of my comfort zone and make me aware of things I've never seen. I want someone who is like the other half of me, who we can bounce ideas off each other to reach the best possible outcome. I want someone who is always down for adventures and decides to actually make plans, instead of just saying he will get around to it when he has time.

I have big hopes and big dreams, but that is because I know that kind of love exists. I know that a love that inspires and gets better with time exists because I've seen it. I've been inspired by it and I want it.

I know it won't come easy. I know I can't just snap my fingers and have it there. Building relationships takes time and being in relationships takes work, but I'm willing to put my all in for a love that inspires me to be better.

The best love is a love that makes you want to be better, without changing who you are to make someone else happy.

Because true love makes you better, it makes you more alive. It makes you more of who you are, not less.

I'll admit I'm a bit of a hopeless romantic, but it's because I know what I want. I want someone who dreams as big as I do. Someone who never wants to live comfortably, but is willing to take risks because they believe that is the way life is supposed to be lived.

I want someone who wants to help me accomplish my goals because I will do that for them. I want someone to challenge me and push me. **I want someone who makes me get lost**

in them. I want someone who makes me dream bigger, who completes the plans in my head, who doesn't make me feel like I'm missing out on anything better and who generally inspires me to be a better person. **And I honestly and completely believe in that type of love.**

28

Girls Don't Want Everything, They Just Want To Be Loved

Over the weekend someone said to me, "He can buy you whatever you want. You should go for him." The first thought that came through my head was *That is not at all what most girls want, and that is definitely not what I want.*

I wasn't interested in him and him having money didn't make me any more interested. What good is a hallow relationship without love and passion?

In the same night I also over heard someone say, "I give her whatever she wants and I buy her everything she asks for. I don't know what else she wants."

Expensive gifts and dinners aren't everything. Money doesn't replace love, money doesn't fill in the gaps of being lonely in a relationship, and money surely doesn't keep you warm at night. Money doesn't make you soup when you're sick, money doesn't hold the umbrella over your head in the rain, and money doesn't make you feel warm and fuzzy inside from passion.

I don't want a relationship that is flooded with gifts that are trying to replace love because love can't be replaced.

Love can't be covered up or overpowered by anything. Love is love and there is nothing more dominant than it.

Love is like magic, sometimes it's impossible to understand or figure out, but no one has to truly understand it other than the ones who are creating the show, as they as they can make it work nothing else matters.

Love makes you feel more alive than anything. It gives you butterflies and makes your heart skip a beat. It makes you nervous, jittery, excited, and passionate. Love makes your heart race and your knees tremble. Love is filling and honest, it is not something that can be replaced or bought.

I want passion. I don't want comfort.

I want to kiss someone like they are the air that fills my lungs, like their kiss is the only thing keeping me alive.

I don't want gifts from someone; I've never wanted gifts. I've never wanted to marry rich so I could live a luxurious lifestyle. I would take being poor and happily in love over being with someone just because they can spoil me. That's not love, and that is not a relationship I'm interested in because money can't buy happiness.

I don't need diamonds and pearls to make me happy, I just want your love. I don't need you to be my hero; I just want you to be there for me. I don't need you to show me off in front of your friends, I just want to feel special to you.

Money can't create feelings that aren't there and sometimes as humans we think that fancy gifts can make up for mistakes or lack of attention, but in all reality, they can't. All women really want is love, attention and to be appreciated.

There is no price tag on giving someone your heart.

Every girl just wants mean something to someone, to feel

a burning passion of love. She wants to give her love and receive it back. She doesn't want to be bought and surrounded by meaningless gifts, she wants to enfolded in your arms and have you reciprocate the nice things she does for you.

Money can't help you solve your problems together, money can't wipe away your tears, and money can't build a solid, happy relationship, **but true love can, and it always does.**

29

I'm Ready To Accept That You'll Never Be My Happily Ever After

As much as it pains me and yanks violently at my heart, I've finally come to terms with it because that's all I can do.

It feels like a giant pill lodged in my throat, and no matter how hard I swallow I can't get rid of the feeling until it's ready to go away itself. It feels like I'm sitting on the dark side of a brand new one-way mirror that I can't get through. So misleading and deceptive because I can see you so clearly on the other side, but you can't see me. I can't touch you. I can't talk to you and as much as I want you to see how much I ache for you; you can't and I don't think you ever will.

On my side, I can see all the endless possibilities of where our lives could lead us, but while I was in front of you the whole time, you couldn't see me. You couldn't open your eyes and see what I saw.

And now you have her.

You're happy with her. She makes you smile and laugh. You talk about her in a way I've never heard you talk about anyone. She lights up your world and I can tell you're happier when she's around.

You do things for her I've never seen you do for anyone, and

I can tell what you have is real by the way you look at her. I can see the way you miss her as soon as you walk her to the front door. It's one of those *I'll miss yous* that chill you to the bone because of the sincerity in your voice.

I tell you I'm happy for you, because I am. I really and truly am.

I've accepted that I'm not going to be the one to kiss your sleepy smile in the morning and tell you it's time to get up for work. I've accepted I won't be the one who gets to call you on your lunch break just to see how your morning went. I've accepted I won't be the one who gets held in your arms at night. I've accepted we won't have a forever and that we probably won't have much of any type of relationship in the future.

But I finally think I'm okay with it.

I'm okay with it because I want someone to look at me the way you look at her. I want someone to love me with every ache and fiber in their body like the way you love her. I want to be *her* to someone. I want to make someone's bad days better and I've finally come to terms that that person isn't you.

Even though I thought I loved you, you never loved me back. You kept looking until you found the one, and then you did.

Now it's my turn to be found, to complete someone else's world and be the reason behind their smile. I don't want to be behind a one-way mirror; I want to be on the other side of a glass where he can see me for what I really am.

This might be the end of *our* story, but it's not the end of mine.

You can't make someone like you. You can't force them to

see you in a romantic way. I truly believe we don't choose who we love, but we do get to choose *how* we love them.

I have to let you go because you love her with all your heart, and the only thing I can do is be happy for you. I'm accepting things cannot be the way I had hoped between us.

You might not be my happily ever after, but someone else will be, and when that day comes I hope you're happy for me, too.

30

This Is The Love I Want To Give Someone

I want to find the person who makes me feel like I found the piece of myself I never knew was missing. I want the nerves and all the good vibes associated with falling for someone new, and when I find that person, I have so much love I want to give to him.

I won't be hesitant, I won't try to be someone I'm not, and I won't try to impress him. I'll just be me, because if he's the right person, that will be enough. Once I find that person, I want to give him all the love in my heart, despite any prior heartache I've felt.

Because I want to give the right person everything I have in me, through the good and the bad.

I'll love you with all my heart and make sure you know you're the only one I care about. I'll make you feel safe and secure around me, like when we're together the world can't touch us. **I'll always keep your promises and won't wager your trust.** I want you to know you can always count on me to be there. I can always promise I'll be the last person you see at night and the first person you see again in the morning, as long as that's what you want.

I'll learn your favorite meals and cook them for you when

you've had a long day. I'll make your morning coffee with mine and cook your eggs exactly the way you like them. I'll become an expert at cooking your favorite dessert, just like your mom does, and if I'm not an expert I'll try until I am. **I'll always smile like a fool when you make me happy.** And I'll always cheer you on when you're trying to accomplish something you've been working for.

I promise I'll try to learn everything about you so I can do the little things every day to show you how much I care.

I want to surprise you with little gifts because they made me think of you. I want to send you a funny YouTube clip because I know it would make you laugh. I want to leave notes around that tell you why I love you or tell you what I want to do to you.

I want to go out of my way to make you happy because your happiness is in fact my happiness.

I'll always offer you the last piece of something and kiss you good morning. I'll always let you share my food with me and tell you "I love you" even when you already know. I'll always ask you about your day and listen your response. **I promise to always laugh at your jokes, even the ones that really aren't funny.** I'll always try to make you laugh and pull you back in the rain to kiss me even though we're both getting soaking wet. I promise I'll sit through your TV shows I hate and will try not to complain. I'll make you soup when you're sick and bring you medicine.

I promise the adventures will never stop and we can continue to explore for as long as we live. I'll never tell you there is a mountain too high for us to climb. I'll always say yes to road trips and be okay with getting lost because you claimed you knew where you were going. I'll love you through all the ups and downs, and bumpy roads we will face.

I won't expect you to be perfect because I know you're not. I know you'll screw up, I know you'll do things that make me want to rip my hair out and I'm positive I'll do those things to you, too. I know we will fight and struggle through hard times because that's life. But on top of all the struggles we face I promise I will always face them with you. **I promise that I won't quit on you when things get hard.** I promise I'll still work through things with you and won't run away from our problems. I'll face them head on with you by my side because that's the only way things will get better.

I'm not saying I'm perfect, but I promise I can be worth it because I'll always give you all the love I have in my heart and love you unconditionally.

31

You Don't Need To Sweep Her Off Her Feet, You Just Need To Ask Her Out

I'm so over Netflix and chill. I'm so done with being asked to watch a movie. I have zero interest in being asked to *hang out*. I don't want you to ask me when I'm free or if I'm bored and want to do something. I don't want any of that.

No one wants to be asked to casually hang out at someone's house the first time they're hanging out alone. That is sleazy and not appealing. I don't want to sit awkwardly on your couch or lay in your bed to watch a movie; if I wanted to do that I could sit on my own couch in the comfort of my own home.

Men, is asking her on a date really that hard to do? Is it that difficult to say, "Would you like to go to dinner with me?" or breakfast, or get coffee, or literally anything that involves plans and going out?

All I want is to be asked out on a proper freaking date and I refuse to think that that is too much to ask.

If I'm spending my time talking to you; obviously I'm interested in you. I don't do it to occupy myself, I don't do it because I'm feeling lonely or bored. I'm not doing it for any reason other than I find you interesting and I want to get to know you better. So, yes, I obviously would like to spend time with you.

When did it become so difficult to pick a time, a date, and a place to meet? We could get ice cream, or lunch, or a beer, or go bungee jumping; hell I'm open to anything. I just want to **actually do something.**

Hiding behind a phone screen or computer screen all day sending witty messages back and forth just isn't good enough for me and it honestly shouldn't be enough for anyone. That isn't a connection; it doesn't allow growth or a relationship to form. The only thing that does is start the process of games and prolonging the far-fetched idea of face-to-face communication and a proper date.

And if you don't want to take me out on a date, **don't talk to me!** Holy shit, a brilliant idea.

I don't want to waste my time and energy trying to seem appealing to someone who doesn't have interest in me. I don't want to try and come up with conversation and interesting topics to talk about. I have other things I'd rather be doing if the relationship is going no where in your mind.

Don't think you're doing me a favor by talking to me instead of ignoring me. Man up and tell me you're not interested; it's as simple as that.

And if you actually are interested, ask me out on a **D A T E.** It's not that hard. Most girls are laid back; they are down to do most things. They just want to know what to wear and how to prepare and they'll be excited you actually took initiative. All they really want is to spend time with you. They want to get to know you and see the kind of person you really are.

Games aren't fun, texting isn't fun, but getting to know a

person face-to-face can be really fun. You can build a way stronger connection in person than you ever can over messaging.

No one wants to be asked to *hang out*. In all honesty, what does that even mean? Ask us out, tell us a date and time, and if we can't make it we will ask you if we can move it. Being asked out is an amazing feeling when someone properly does it. **It means he is serious. It means he is actually interested and he has confidence.** Which is AMAZING.

I'm not asking you to buy me a house. I'm not asking you to cook me a gourmet meal or show up doing back flips.

All I'm asking is for you to show up, to ask me out on a date.

If it doesn't go well, you move on. If it goes well, great, we can see where it goes. Either way a date isn't going to kill you.

No one likes rejection, but I can almost guarantee if she has been spending time talking to you and throwing out hints, there is almost a one hundred percent chance she will go out with you. So man up and ask her on the date already! She will automatically think more of you.

32

Ladies, There's A Difference Between Guys Liking You And Valuing You

There is absolutely a difference between liking someone and valuing them. Sometimes I think we get more concerned with the fact that someone *likes* us that we forget how important it is to be *valued*. Being liked is good, but being valued is so much better.

I like my phone. It occupies me when I'm bored, I can use it as a distraction, and it normally does what I say, but I wouldn't say I necessarily value it. I drop it, I break it, and as soon as it's broken I start asking my friends if they have old phones I could replace mine with. It's just a phone. It's great when it's working, but once it stops and has problems I look to replace it or upgrade to something new and better.

That is the difference between liking and valuing, and that difference is major.

Don't be with someone because they string pretty little words together that make you feel special if their actions don't match up.

Don't just stand around on the side waiting for a guy

because he tells you he like you, but follows that line with an excuse about how he isn't ready yet for anything.

Don't waste precious days of your life trying to capture his attention because honestly, you don't want to be hung up on a guy who keeps you hanging around because he might like you. **You don't deserve someone who just likes you; you deserve someone who values you.**

You deserve someone who knows just how important you are and how much you're worth. You should be the highlight of someone's life, someone's better half, and the part of them that makes them want to be better. You should be that person to someone because a person's values are usually one of the most important things to them.

You deserve to not be taken for granted.

To be valued means that you are appreciated for your role in his life. It means that he respects you and how you feel. It means he doesn't belittle you, he doesn't make your accomplishments seem small, and **he doesn't kick you to the curb when something better comes along.** He truly cares about you because he cares about your values and beliefs.

Your values should be everything to you and more important than a guy liking you.

You can claim to be strong in your values, but it's important to realize the company you keep says a lot about how you value yourself.

By hanging around someone who doesn't value you, it's showing others you don't value yourself as much as you should.

Because if you're hanging out with someone who doesn't value you, it's changing your values, not theirs.

If you live your life with the values of trust, respect, and love, you shouldn't settle for someone who doesn't fully invest in you and your relationship. You shouldn't be with someone who doesn't fully trust, respect, or love you just because you're scared to let him go in hopes he might change. **All that is doing is compromising your values and internally diminishing your self-worth.**

You can't constantly wonder what you're doing wrong or why he isn't as invested in you as you are him when you've let your values down in order to let him in. You want to be the change; you hope you can be the change in him, but love is not meant to change a person into who you want them to be. Love can't change your partner and make them into someone they're not.

You have to know your value in order to be treated right.

A man can like you, but that doesn't mean he will show you the respect you need and deserve. Sometimes you just need to start from where you are with some self-love and care. You need to invest in yourself with a little maintenance, then you will start to see your value build back up again over time. Then you will see how important you are.

Know your worth and practice your values before someone else can come in and start compromising them.

33

I Know I Can't Have You, But I Still Crave Your Touch

La Douleur Exquise [French]: **The heart-wrenching pain of wanting someone you can't have.**

I tell myself over and over again how bad it is to want you. I think of you in ways I haven't thought about anyone in a long time. When I see you I get tongue-tied and filled with butterflies. You make me nervous, in a good way. All I can think about is that night and I instantly want your lips on mine again. I want you to wrap your arms around me and pull me in. I want you to whisper sweet nothings in my ear and then tell me how much you want me right after.

I want all of that and I want you, but I know I can't have you.

I can't have you because you're not mine to have. You've never been mine. You were just like a waterfall I stopped to admire on my path ahead, but instead of only admiring your beauty I feel in and got swept away while you kept flowing into the same pond.

You sucked me in and now you have me hooked. I'm yours for the taking, but you won't have me.

You won't have me because you have her.

I know it was a one-night kind of thing; it was just one little kiss, a harmless kiss that nothing will come from. But all it took was one little kiss that got me hooked. I tell myself over and over again that it can't happen again, that it won't happen. I've come to realize this and I've slowly been telling myself I have to accept things as they are.

I keep telling myself you're not the one I want, but like the saying goes, *We always want what we can't have.* And all I want is you.

I crave your touch, I want your hands on my body, I've wanted you since the moment our eyes locked and I first saw you. You drew me in. You've become the itch I can't scratch, the glue I can't peel off, the scab I keep picking at. You've begun to consume me and as much as I want you, I hate you for that.

I hate you for coming into my life. I hate you for pulling me in. I hate you for the sweet words that came out of your mouth. I hate you for the thoughts you put in my head. But of all the things I've come to hate about you, I hate myself more, for hating you, for giving in to you and for wanting you.

But as much hate as I feel, I know it won't do anything because when the sun goes down, you're still in my head, and part of me still hopes if there was a next time you'd pick me.

For now, I'll just think of you. I'll remember your words and cherish your touch because as much as I want you, I know I can't have you. Not this time, anyway.

34

You Deserve To Be The Most Important Person To Someone, No Matter What

You deserve to be the first thing someone thinks about in the morning. You deserve to feel completely and truly wanted. You deserve someone to eat pizza and ice cream in bed with you when you're having a rough day. **You deserve someone to pull the car up to the curb when it's pouring rain, even if that means they get soaked.** You deserve someone who actually, truly, and completely gives a shit about you. Someone who returns your phone calls and answers your texts, not someone whose attention you have to repeatedly beg for.

You deserve someone who thinks about you all the time. You deserve someone who cares about you enough to worry when they haven't heard from you all day. **You deserve someone you can count on and rely on when things get tough.** You deserve someone to watch your favorite TV shows with. You deserve someone who is committed to you. You deserve someone who thinks you're sexy in sweatpants. You deserve someone who genuinely cares how your day went.

You deserve someone who will hold the door open for you,

but still smack your ass as you walk by. You deserve someone who will whisper sweet words into your ear but also talk dirty to you. You deserve someone who wants you in every way imaginable, who loves you unconditionally, and is head over heels in love you with. You deserve to be the most important person in the world to someone. You deserve to be the person they couldn't imagine living without.

Because everyone, and I mean everyone, deserves someone to keep them looking for tomorrow.

To keep them looking forward to better things and keep them excited about life. Everyone deserves that type of love and happiness. I don't care who you are or what you've done, but you deserve to feel like you matter and you deserve to have someone give a shit about you.

Life is hard, and life can surely suck sometimes, but it's a hell of a lot better with someone you can count on by your side.

Love makes the world go round, love is the strongest force to reckon with, and love is the most powerful weapon.

You deserve to be the most important person to someone because life isn't meant to be tackled on your own. Life is meant to be filled with laughter and kindness, generosity and hope, and a passion for others.

Everyone deserves to be someone's *yes* instead of someone's *maybe*. Everyone deserves to be pursued and to feel wanted. **Everyone deserves to be a priority, not just an option.** Everyone deserves all this and more because life is meant to be shared with those you love and cherish.

There is no such thing as too much love. If you love someone, tell them; they deserve it. They deserve to know how much you care about them and what you're feeling. Even if you've told them a thousand times, tell them a thousand more because they deserve to hear it.

Everyone deserves love. Everyone deserves to feel important. Everyone deserves to feel like they matter. And everyone deserves to be the most important person to someone.

Everyone deserves that magic.

35

I'm Still Single Because I'm Too Scared To Take Risks

All my life I've lived on the adventurous side; normalcy bores me to no end. I get in a bad mood after a few days of routine without any thrill or excitement. I've always been outgoing and a risk taker when it comes to life. **But when it comes to my love life, it is the complete opposite.**

I'm completely certain I've been single this long because of me, because of who I am as a person. I judge people too quickly based on their first impressions to know well in advance that I wouldn't want a future with them or even that I wouldn't want to try. I put them in the friend zone where they will live the rest of their lives.

I'm a friend kind of girl; I downloaded a dating app and I've made friends on it. When someone tries to flirt with me I'll instantly call him 'dude' or something that makes guys cringe to hear.

I'll make out with people on the weekend then disregard them during the week because as into them as I might have been when I'm drunk, **I have way too much pride to crave them when I'm sober.** I won't try to create something out of it; I try to shut it down as fast as I can. It's just not me and it has been who I've been for a long time.

I've never wanted to be the needy girl or the emotional girl who needs attention from men.

I'm the strong girl, the one who doesn't give a fuck about love.

I'm the one who tells her friends she doesn't need to talk to a douchebag just because she's lonely. I tell my friends they deserve better; I tell them the things they don't want to hear or accept because they hate feeling alone. I like to stand my ground and be tough. I like my sense of pride and I like even more feeling like I don't need anyone and can take perfect care of myself.

But what I'm coming to realize is that I'm single because I'm scared to take risks. I cover everything up with a false sense of security that I give myself.

I'm scared to let someone know me on a romantic level. I'm scared to let someone into my life in fear that they will leave. I'm nervous and terrified that I won't be good enough for someone after spending time with them.

I'll rarely, if ever, approach a guy at the bar and attempt to flirt with him. I won't go up and start grinding on someone on the dance floor. I won't twirl my hair and play dumb. I won't wear shirts that my boobs are nearly hanging out of because that isn't me and I don't think I need the attention.

When in reality, I think it's time for me to accept that I don't throw myself out there because I'm scared of rejection.

I lack the self-confidence that they will never pick me; I always assume they will pick her.

Whoever *her* is, she must be better than I am. That's just how my brain works.

I know it's not right; I know I have guys that try to talk to me, but instead of giving them the chance I shut them down. **I stick them in the friend zone because at least I know they're safe there.** At least I know they have less of a chance to hurt me while they're there.

I fall easily for people but only for people who I don't have a chance with. They're just little crushes I keep in my mind. **It's nothing real, and that way it doesn't have the potential to hurt me.**

I don't know if I'll ever be the girl who isn't scared to take risks. I think part of me will always be the girl who is too scared of rejection so I'll just hang in the back. I'll accept that I'll always be the girl with lots of guy friends because I'm more scared to take the risk and wind up losing them than just having them in my life as friends.

I've come to realize I am my own problem, but I also know I can be my own solution. One day the risk taking will come, one day when I'm ready. **Until then, welcome to the friend zone boys.**

36

All I Want Is A Real, Raw And Imperfect Everyday Kind Of Love Story

I don't want a fairytale love. I don't want a pathway constructed of petals and candles leading me to a prince on a bed. I don't want a knight in shinning armor. I don't want someone to swoop in and save me. I don't want a rare fiction love story.

I want an everyday love story with someone who likes getting just as drunk as I do.

I want a love story where we come home from the bar and stuff our faces with pizza.

When I'm hungover and rolling around in bed complaining about my headache, all I want is my boyfriend to be a little less hung over so he can get me pain reliever and a bagel.

I want someone who tells me I'm annoying when I'm complaining, because I know I can be. I want someone who messes around with me for a little bit, only to make their point, then leaves me alone to suffer the rest of the day.

I want a real love, a flawed love, and an imperfect love.

I want someone who isn't afraid to embarrass me on the dance floor and sing his heart out on the car ride home. I want someone who isn't into slow dancing at concerts but into having a good time with our whole group of friends, just like I do. **I want someone who grabs my hand and tells me we're going to do something, even if I fight and say I don't want to, because he knows once I do it the first time I'll be hooked.**

I want someone who I can sit at the other end of the table with our friends and have normal conversation, laughing at everything while still having inside jokes. I want to make faces at each other and tell embarrassing stories about shit no one wants revealed but we still find it hilarious.

I don't want a proper, sophisticated, well-mannered boyfriend because I am sure as hell not a proper, sophisticated, well-mannered girl.

I want someone who is weird with me, someone who not only accepts my quirks but embraces them because he has his own. I want someone who is compatible to my weirdness and humor. I want someone who laughs at dirty, inappropriate jokes because as fucked up as they are, they are still undeniably hard not to laugh at.

I don't need good morning texts or breakfast in bed. I'd rather crawl out of bed with him in the morning and decide we should just go to McDonald's drive thru breakfast because we're lazy and don't feel like cooking.

I don't need someone to surprise me with front row seats to an NFL game, and I just want to go with them and get rowdy with our friend group in the parking lot before hand with lots of snacks and booze. I want to cheer together and high five each other after a touchdown.

I don't need the romantic shit because frankly, I'm not a romantic person.

I don't want someone who is going to read my poetry and

write me love songs. I don't need someone who wants to lift me off my feet and carry me away to a castle.

I don't need fairytales and I don't need fancy. I want the good, the bad and the ugly because that's life, and sooner or later you're going to fight. You have to fight because fighting is healthy. I don't want to change him, but I want to yell at him if he needs to stop doing something that is upsetting me, just like he better do the same to me.

I want someone who can laugh at me and my jokes, someone who can push me and make me think, and someone who tells me I'm being stupid when I'm trying to do too much.

I don't want someone who is perfect, and I definitely don't want to pretend I'm perfect to get someone. I want someone who I know isn't perfect but is perfect for me in our own little fucked up ways.

37

I Keep Touching Your Fire As If This Time It Won't Burn

I keep going back to you even when I know it isn't worth it. I tell myself to stay away, but I've never been one to take my own advice.

You've become the quicksand I keep thinking I can make it through, as if I haven't already been sucked down before. You've become the beehive I keep poking at, as if this time I'll be able to out run the bees before I get stung. You've become the fire I keep touching, as if this time it won't burn me as badly.

I know what I'm getting myself into, but for some reason I keep telling myself that things will be different this time. Even though I already know the outcome, I still can't help myself.

I tell you I don't want to talk to you because it's easier to lie to you than to myself.

I tell you I'm not interested because I want you to think I'm strong and I don't need you, but in reality I lie awake in bed hoping you're thinking of me, too. I tell you I don't want to talk to you because I'm trying to convince myself that's the right thing to do, even though I'd give anything for one more night with you by my side. I tell you it's better this way, to go our own ways, but secretly I hope for your call to tell me you miss me, too.

You're the tornado and I'm the storm chaser that hangs around a little too long and gets sucked up by you every time for admiring your destruction.

I know you're bad for me. I know I should walk away. I know the outcome will always remain the same, but I'm desperate for you. I crave your touch, I cherish your words, and I yearn for a world where we're good for each other.

I naïvely think that this time it will get better, that maybe you will have changed and things will work between us this time. But it never gets better. It's always the same burn, the same let down and the same feeling of insanity because nothing ever changes. Yet I still expect a different result every time I start lingering back to you.

I know it's time I stop reaching through the same fence and allowing the same dog to bite my hand just like I've let him do so many times before. But now it's become a game, the same game I've been losing for years.

I'm waiting for the day where I can reach my hand in the fire and realize this time it doesn't burn.

But if that day never comes, I just hope I learn before I'm covered in burns that will always remind me of you.

38

I'll Hate Myself In The Morning, But I'll Love You All Night

I see you staring at me from across the bar. For a split second I try to convince myself to walk away. I tell myself it isn't worth it, that *you're* not worth it. I tell myself I'll hate myself in the morning. As much as I know that it's true, I don't stop walking your way. Your coy little smile always draws me in and I can't resist you anymore.

I know you're not good for me; everyone in the room can see that. I should just turn around, head in the other direction, not give you the time of day. But I'm not strong enough to break the tension between us, especially not after a few drinks.

You've become all I want. You've shattered all the strength I've managed to build up because I can't turn you down.

I want to run my fingers through your hair and wake up by your side entangled in sheets and regret because regret always follows. Every time.

We know it won't work between us, but we keep stupidly trying. We both know we're not good for each other, but you've turned into the one person who I can't resist. You're the one I can't help but want even though I know things will never work out in our favor.

Because the fire keeps burning between us and we can't put it out no matter how hard we try; you're the gasoline and I always catch like wildfire.

I want you; I want all of you, even though I shouldn't have you, even though I *can't* have you. I tell myself *Just one more time.* I tell myself I'll walk away from you next time because there won't be a next time. I tell myself I'll finally start listening to the voice in my head trying to convince me to walk away. I'll do it in the morning when I once again open my eyes and feel my body fill with regret, because I know I'll hate myself in the morning, but I'm still going to love you all night.

I'm convinced one more time won't hurt because I want to be wrapped in your arms. I want to feel your lips on mine. I want to feel your hands on my face. I want to feel close to you. I want to give in to you again because as wrong as it is, it also feels so right, **so I do.**

I know you're a bad decision before I make it, but you and I are like bees and pollen. We always find each other and once we do, there's no stopping us.

Leaving us behind is going to be hard, but I'm making a promise to myself that the last time was the last time and as tempted as I am, there won't be a next time. We owe it to ourselves to move on **because I'm tired of hating myself in the morning from loving you all night.**

39

Date Someone Who Loves Your Belly

Date someone who loves you for who you are. Don't date someone who wants to change you because they might not *love* the way you look completely. Don't put yourself through that torture always trying to be good enough for them. Don't make someone else's opinion about your body change the way you see yourself in a negative manner.

Be proud of your body, and if you want to work on changing it, do it because you love yourself, not because you hate your body. And make sure everything you do you do for you.

You are worth so much more than your body weight and the number on a scale.

If he likes you he likes you for you. The first-time you hook up with the right guy he won't look at you and say, "Ah, never mind, I thought you were five pounds lighter." No. That won't happen because he likes you for who you are, not for your weight.

And in the rare, fucked up case that does happen, he isn't the right kind of guy, anyway. You don't want to be with someone that shallow and down right rude. **Don't allow him to diminish your self-worth and shatter your self-love.** That is his own problem he needs to spend time working on and fixing.

Date someone who loves your belly, who loves to rest his head on your little pudge.

Date someone who will gladly sit down and eat a bowl of ice cream with you before bed because he knows how much you love ice cream. Date someone who loves to show you off, even if you're not a size two. **Date someone who is completely and utterly obsessed with you in every way.**

Date someone who thinks your rolls are cute when you sit down and loves the way your belly moves when you start laughing uncontrollably. Date someone who falls in love with what you consider your flaws. Date someone who loves how your belly feels against his arm when you're cuddling in bed.

Date someone who wouldn't change a thing about your body even if he could but fully supports you if you want to make your own changes. Date someone who cares about your health, someone who wants you to be healthy because they care about your actual well-being. Don't date someone who forces you to eat healthy because they want you to look like a super model.

Date someone who loves your body, who supports you, and who treats you right. Date someone who is proud of you when you go to the gym and achieve one of your fitness goals, but also date someone who is proud of you when you can eat more pizza than him because you're really hungry and feel like pigging out.

Don't let a man influence your body image. Don't let him make you feel bad about your choices and take away what you love. There is a difference between healthy and starving yourself to please someone.

So please, never change for anyone. Your body image should never define you because you are worth so much more than the number on a scale.

40

Part Of You Will Always Live In Me, And I'm At Peace With That

You're not going to be the one I meet at the end of the aisle to say 'I do,' you're not going to be the one I have my first dance with, and you're not going to be the one who I spend my 'forever' with. That's not you.

But a piece of you will always be with me through every step of my life, because part of you will always live in me.

I'll always think back to the days I used to be so reckless. I'll think back to all the times I snuck out of my parents' house to meet you late at night. I'll think of all the dirt roads we called our own. **I'll think of all the long talks we shared because neither of us wanted to go home.** I'll think of all the times we almost got caught doing whatever it was at a given time. But I'll also think of all the times I still wasn't what you wanted, and you were still never enough for me because we both wanted different things.

The way you made me feel was inexplicable; it was like sticking my finger in an electric socket. I knew it would sting, but I wanted to do it anyway for the pleasure and the thrill.

There was no denying we were bad for each other. We used

each other, we tormented each other, and we fought with each other, yet we still loved each other for so many years.

Every time one of us would step away, the other came crawling back.

We were each other's own personal form of cocaine.

Each time we thought we were strong enough to give it up and walk away, the urge came back and we took another hit.

It has finally been years, nearly four to be exact. **I've been clean from you.** I've moved on and walked away for good. You no longer hold any power over me, but as much as I used to implore your touch, the urge is gone; it's long gone.

But the memories haven't washed away into the vast ocean yet. They're still lingering on the shore, waiting for a big enough storm to come and wash them all away, even though I'm still uncertain if there even is a big enough storm capable of doing that.

You'll always be one of my best memories, even through the questions, the love, and the animosity.

You made me feel everything when I was around you, and from that you made me feel alive.

I've come to accept that we weren't meant to end up together, even through four years of constant back and forth, between dating others and still desiring each other. You were the first one who stole my heart, and part of me still believes you hold a little piece of it because part of you still lives in me.

I'll always remember your bright blue eyes and the way they looked at me. I'll always remember the way you made me feel. I have yet to meet another who has made me feel like you did. I'll always remember your crooked smile when you'd look down, and I'll always remember the way you loved me.

I'll keep the good memories close to my heart, because our time is long gone now. I think I've finally come to peace with our past and accepted that the past is exactly where you belong.

41

Read This If It Feels Like Everyone Around You Is Finding Love (Except For You)

I know it might not be everyone—I know it isn't everyone—but it sure as hell feels like it.

I'm happy for everyone who is finding love—that isn't sarcasm either. I'm genuinely excited for my friends who have been finding love lately because I know they're actually happy. They've found someone who makes them happy.

But while they're happy and word vomit is flowing out of their mouths like lava about their new loves, I'm still alone.

I have no one to go on dinner dates with. I have no one to spend lazy Sundays watching movies with. I have no one to just go fuck around with when I'm bored. I have no one to talk to late into the night. I have no one to touch or sleep next to. I have no one to kiss good night or good morning.

I have no one to learn.

I have no one to love.

I have no one that makes me feel that pure bliss that seemingly everyone around me is feeling, and that is enough to make me feel alone.

I can watch movies on my own on Sundays, but that doesn't mean I want to. I can get into my car and go for a drive; I can call a friend and see if they want to go get lost on some roads we've never been down. But I'd rather have someone to get lost with and explore with; someone to feel comforted by, holding his hand as we turn down the curvy roads singing our hearts out side by side. I can swipe left and right all night on my phone and try to make small talk, but I'd rather have someone by my side, a real someone who cares about the words coming out of my mouth.

I want someone to miss, I want someone's hand to hold, and I want someone to love with every once in me.

I want to share the love in my heart; I want to be crazy in love and happy. I want the sparks, the fireworks, the comfort, the reliability, the happiness, the fighting, and more than anything, a best friend.

I want a best friend to do everything with, someone that makes me feel like I've found my perfectly compatible weirdo to share my life with.

I don't want much, hell I'm not going to ask for anything other than someone who cares about me. I don't care if we live out of an RV. I don't care how much money we have. I don't care where we live in the world. **The only thing I actually care about is how you love me.**

It's extremely hard to watch everyone else around me fall in love; it makes me feel painfully alone. It makes me want to stand on top of a roof top and scream, "When is it my turn?!" It feels like I'm due for a relationship, I feel like I've been patiently waiting, not looking for love, doing my own thing, being just fine on my own, but I'm still alone. I've still got nothing.

As happy as I am for my friends, it's also hard to always be happy for someone else when you just want to be happy yourself.

But I know my time will come and one day someone might look up to my relationship and say, "I wish I had that."

Until then, I'll just keep smiling and listening to their stories, I'll keep telling them I'm happy for them and keep bottling up my loneliness because I know some day I won't feel so alone, and I can't wait for that day.

42

I'm Sorry For Acting Like I'm Always Getting My Heart Broken

I'm sorry for always playing the victim, for acting like I always get broken and I never do the breaking. **Because honestly, I do the breaking a lot more than I get broken.**

I shut guys out; I might tease them a little bit only to reject them. I feel bad about not answering, but I do it because I don't have the guts to say, "This is why I don't like you…" and give them a degrading list of things that they can't control because I'm picky.

I suck as a person. I won't try to deny that.

I'm not perfect. I don't claim to be and I don't try to be, but there is another side of the heartbreak story, and that's the side where I do the heart breaking.

To all the men who came into my life who I couldn't want back: know that I tried. I always tried to give you a chance. I saw the best in you, but there was something about you that just wouldn't let me see past that moment. It wouldn't let me see a future with you; I didn't want to see a future with you. So I moved on, I left you in the dust, I didn't check in to see how you were doing, I just moved on because I wanted something different or I wanted someone who I thought was better. I did it without disregard to your feelings and for that I'm sorry.

Girls always love to play the heartbroken one. We get our hearts broken and we blame in on the guys because it's easier that way. I've gotten my heart broken plenty of times for not being wanted back, so I understand your struggle and have felt your pain. But we don't realize it so much until it's happening to us.

When we don't like you our feelings are detached, we think there is no way you could be attached because we aren't. So we just leave, maybe you get a reason or an explanation, or maybe you don't. I guess it depends how important you were to us.

But all I really want to say is I'm sorry. I'm sorry for acting like a bitch. I'm sorry for making you fall for me, even though it was probably unintentional because me attempting to flirt is like a bird flying into a windshield: it never ends well.

I'm sorry for all of it. I'm sorry for sleeping with you and not responding to your Snapchats anymore, I'm sorry for making promises and bailing, and I'm sorry for being a shitty person and being selfish. I'm sorry I wanted so much from you to give you nothing but loneliness in return.

I'm so fucking sorry.

I'll try to be better. I'll try not to do the same thing in the future, but I don't know if I can. You can try to force your heart to like someone as much as you want, but it doesn't mean it's going to happen and sometimes I think we forget that.

We get upset when we get rejected, but we laugh at others when we reject them. We sit around and gossip about what a loser that guy was as we're stuffing our faces with pizza. Girls can be really fucking mean and I'm sorry for that, too. It's a sad and painful cycle.

But more than anything, I'm sorry for acting like I'm always getting my heart broken when I know you would have loved me unconditionally, and I'm sorry I couldn't love you back.

43

You Used To Be My Sun, But My World Is Just As Bright Without You

You used to be my universe. I felt like I couldn't breathe without you by my side, but I guess that's what happens when you fall in love for the first time.

You drop everything in life and cling to them because you don't know any better. You don't have the skepticism and you don't know the pain. You don't have any guards up and instead you have open arms ready to grab at him and pull him in close. You want to smother him in your love because you have a full heart with only a few dings and bangs, but it's not broken and you aren't missing any pieces.

I was utterly obsessed with you. You were my sun; when you shined I shined. We were inseparable and I couldn't imagine my life without you.

But you burned out; you left me in the dark with nothing but sadness and memories.

My darkness was deep, but you didn't notice because you had already moved on. You left me there alone, scared, hopeless, and a mess. **You knew I was scared of the dark, but you didn't care** because you went out and found another girl who needed you to be her sun.

I didn't think I'd ever be able to pull myself together; I didn't think I'd be able to stop the tears. **I didn't think I'd ever be able to find the light again, but I did.**

Now my sun isn't a person. I'm done giving someone that honor until I know they can handle it. You did exactly what I should have known you would do all along, but I was too young and too naïve. That comes with your first love, though; I've learned now. I gave you everything I had in me and you took most of it. But now, on my own, I found my strength again.

My world is bright again. I made it shine on my own.

I'm still more skeptical now; I judge guys because I know what they're capable of. I know what they're after most of the time, but I know what I'm after, too.

Loving you hurt me, it broke me, and it made me realize the pain I could feel when I make someone my whole world. But I don't think I'll ever regret loving you.

You taught me a lot. Not so much at the time, but after. **When I was alone, when I was *forced* to be alone, I learned a lot about myself.** I learned who I was with you and who I wanted to be after.

I am a different person now than before I loved you. I am no longer pure and hopeful. I am damaged and broken. But I found strength in that. I found the person I want to be.

You might have been my sun, but now my world still shines without you.

You were the most important thing to me at one point, but now I'm the most important thing to myself. So I thank you for that. I'm glad I loved you. I'm glad I got to experience love and loss.

But more than anything, I'm glad I got to discover that I don't need someone else to be my world because my world is still whole on my own.

44

Thank You For Being Honest (Even If The Rejection Stings)

There are a lot of things I wish I could say to you. A lot of words I would have tried to use to hurt you because you hurt me, but I could never get them out of my mouth.

I stayed silent, I said, "Okay, if that's what you want."

I let you go because I figured if you wanted me than you would come back, you would have realized you made a mistake, but you never came back. I'm still the one who tries to reach out, if anything. I stay hopeful and I always try to think the best of people even after the hurt me, because I think maybe just maybe they'll realize I was the one who got away. Maybe, *just maybe,* I'd be the one they realize they missed the opportunity to love, but it hasn't happened yet.

I'm still alone and they're still doing their own thing. That's the hard part: no one comes back—no one ever comes back—and if they do make an attempt to come back, they never own up for walking away. They never own up for not giving us a chance, they just send a Snapchat or they favorite some tweets. They do subtle things to grab my attention and it works, but I won't go back.

Then you came along, a straight shooter. You were never about the bullshit.

You were honest and you didn't care if it hurt me to know the truth because you figured it was better to know what's going on than pretend that everything is okay. You always thought that made more sense, to be up front than to hurt someone from behind, and as painful as that felt at the time, I'm forever grateful for that. I'm so thankful that you were honest with me, even though it hurt.

With you, I didn't have to sit around questioning where I went wrong. I didn't have to wonder if it was all the words I said or maybe all the words I didn't say. I didn't wonder if you found someone else to occupy your spare time and I was old news. **I normally just wondered, my mind filled with questions I never got the answers to.** But you eased the pain, you cushioned the blow, you told me what was up, and you gave me the reassurance that I needed.

When you told me you weren't ready, that there was still someone else lingering in your mind, I was happy almost. I felt relief. I felt like as much as it hurt me to hear, I was happy. I wished you the best, I thanked you for your honesty, and I let you go. **I didn't beat myself up for what I could have done better.** I didn't torment myself with questions of where I went wrong. I simply understood I had to let you go because if I kept clinging on it would have only made you resent me.

Thank you for rejecting me. It might have hurt, but it didn't hurt as much as silence. It didn't hurt as much as staring at my phone with a lump in my throat wondering why I haven't heard back from you. It didn't hurt as much as getting ignored and feeling used to ease a time of loneliness for someone.

Rejection hurts, but it feels a hell of a lot better than silence does.

Thank you for your honesty. That right there proves you cared enough about me and makes me feel like it wasn't all a waste.

45

I Was So Excited About The Potential Of Us

I lay awake in bed at night with thoughts of you crowding my head. I've nearly given up on trying to push them away because it feels like there is no point anymore.

The more I try to forget the more you're there.

I let the thoughts swallow me as I think about all that we could have been.

I hate to admit it, but **I hate how deeply I miss what we almost had.**

You were different. You were someone I didn't get bored of; you were someone I wanted more of. You were someone I could actually see myself sticking with, but you obviously didn't feel the same about me. I thought there was potential that you could be the one, but potential doesn't mean anything if you don't do anything with it.

I tried to hold on, but you pulled away, and it felt like the tighter I grabbed, the faster you ran.

I really think we were meant to be, but we did it wrong. Maybe in another life or if our paths cross again in the future, maybe our hearts will align. **Or maybe I'll realize what a fool I'd been all this time.** I know it might sound crazy, but there really was something different about you that made it so hard to let you go.

I thought you were different and that makes me a fool. I swore you were different; I convinced myself things were different and that you weren't who everyone warned me about. But as usual, they were right. You weren't different, but you made me feel different. You made me feel things I never thought I could. Maybe that's why it's making goodbye so hard.

It's stopping me from letting go and forcing me to cling to everything I never thought I could.

We were never in love, but do I believe we had the potential to fall hard.

Maybe that scared you so you ran; you weren't ready to feel something real. Or maybe you just couldn't picture your forever with a girl like me. You left and now I'm stuck with all the memories of the good times we shared, unable to reach out and call you, unable to touch your hand, and unable to make anymore memories. So I cling to what I've got; I cling to the memories of 'us' and come to terms with the fact that I'll now only have memories of what we could have been.

If you taught me anything from leaving it's that I need to stop believing in the idea of what could have been. I need to let go and move on, without you, just like you did without me.

I need to stop clinging to the potential, because even if I did find the right person, it wasn't the right time for you.

I could wish you the worst, hope you're haunted by what we could have been and wished you'd realized what you left behind, but you already know that. You knew what we could have been and the way I could have loved you, but you decided you wanted something different, and that is okay, too.

I was so excited about the potential of us, but there is no 'us' and there is no more potential. So I'm deciding to let you go and stop believing in what could have been.

46

14 Things To Expect When You Date A Girl With A Big Personality

1. You might disagree, a lot.

She has a strong mind and stronger opinions. There will be times she's convinced she's right and you're wrong. Sometimes you just have to swallow your pride and accept that you'd rather be happy than right.

2. She doesn't like things sugar coated.

She doesn't want you to make excuses or beat around the bush. She wants you to come out and tell her what's going on. She doesn't like games and she's not into drama, so be honest with her.

3. She will constantly try to motivate you.

She likes when she feels she is in control and she loves success. She will try her hardest to make sure that you are motivated, too. She has goals and dreams and she wants to reach them, but she also wants to help you reach yours along the way.

4. She is confident.

She is confident in herself and her decisions. If she make a poor decision along the way she will own up for it and make it right. Her confidence glows off of her and it's aiding in her success as a person.

5. She's all about new experiences and adventures.

A girl with a big personality is big on life. She loves to try new things and experience as much of the world as she can. She rarely says no because her passion and adventure seeking thrill has been around a lot longer than you. So strap up and enjoy the trip.

6. She likes meaningful conversation.

She loves connections and she only feels like she's getting those connections when she's having a deep conversation with someone. She has no time for small talk in her life.

7. Just because she might not agree with you doesn't mean your opinion is irrelevant.

Even though she doesn't agree with some things she will always at least give you the chance to speak your mind. She is open to interpretation on the topic, but most of the time she just believes in what she believes in and there is no changing that.

8. She will always try to give you the best advice.

She is fairly levelheaded and loves when people come to her for help. She might not always know what to do in every situation, but she will try her best to try to figure out some type of solution for you.

9. She can be stubborn as hell.

She doesn't mean to be, but she can't help it. A girl with a big personality is set in her ways. She knows what she likes and she wants it that way.

10. She's not a huge fan of 'down time.'

She gets bored easily and hates being unproductive. She can't sit around on the couch all day without feeling like she wasted the day. She hates sleeping until 11 AM because it makes her feel lazy. She likes having a schedule and getting things done.

11. She's very competitive.

Like I said, she hates being wrong, but she also hates losing. She wants to be the best at everything, even things that seem impossible. If she's participating, she wants to win.

12. She will defend everything and everyone she loves.

She won't let you come in and start bashing anything she's passionate about. She will always stand up for what she believes in and she doesn't care if she's the only one in the room who feels a certain way, she will make it known.

13. The girl with a big personality also has a big heart.

She truly cares about other people and loves everyone. While she is tough, she is also very emotional. She wants the best for those she cares about and she has a passion for the world burning in her heart.

14. She will love you unconditionally.

When she makes a commitment to something she will fully commit. She will put her whole heart and soul into loving you because she will expect you give her all your love right back. She will be faithful and honest because that's just the kind of person she is.

47

This Is What I Want So Desperately To Say (Even When I'm Being The 'Cool Girl')

Everyone likes the 'cool girl,' the girl who just hangs around drinking her beer. The girl who avoids the drama and instead hangs out with the guys. The girl who bites her tongue instead of getting mad and starting a fight. The girl who doesn't ever act too interested but always laughs even if she doesn't understand the joke. She just kind of chills because that's what she does. She's the 'cool girl' who doesn't get bothered by anything and can take a joke and give it right back.

She's the dream girl.

I've tried to be the 'cool girl.' I try to lay back and just go with the flow. I try to be cute while smart but cool and interesting while being interested in the conversation all at the same time. I try to sit tight and have a go with the boys, just being one of the guys.

I try not to act too interested when I'm talking to someone new because if you act too interested it's a turn off. No one wants someone easy, everyone loves a chase so I try to seem vague. I try to seem like I'm interested, but not THAT interested. I try to create desire and a bit of curiosity when in all actuality I just want to say, "I like your smile and I think you're funny, date me."

But you can't do that.

That's not cool or desirable. No one wants someone who is that upfront because where is the fun in that?

I wish I could walk right up to you and tell you that I think about you constantly, that I barely know you, but I want to know so much more. I wish I could walk right up to you, grab your face and kiss you on the mouth. I wish I could tell you how I want you to wrap your arms around me and pull me in close. I wish I could tell you I want to jump on a plane and go get lost in some foreign destination with only you by my side.

But you can't do that.

You become pathetic and desperate. You become a stage five clinger and everyone runs for the hills. We start to feel all these emotions, but we're meant to hide them.

We're supposed to tuck our feelings away deep down and suppress our emotions because no one wants someone who is that honest and open. It scares the shit out of us.

So, we all try to be that person: the 'cool girl.' The girl who doesn't think deeply into things but just lets them happen. We try to be the girl who doesn't have too many emotions or feelings because that would make us crazy. When we're jealous we act like we're not upset that he's more interested in another girl than us. We try to act like we don't want to know everything about him; we try to act like we didn't get upset when we didn't get a text back. **We try to be cool; we try to be someone we're not.**

It sucks, and it sucks big. I so desperately want to tell you that you've been on my mind, that I can't stop thinking about you, and I want to know you from the inside out. But you can't. You can't open up like that until you're actually dating and comfortable. You have to act like you're less you and more 'cool girl' from the start so he is into you.

We cover up pieces of ourselves and unveil them little by little until he can finally see there is no such thing as the 'cool girl' because we're all a little bit crazy.

I'm trying to be the 'cool girl' for you. There is so much more I desperately want to say, but I won't. Not yet anyway.

48

If You Don't Love All Of Her, Let Her Go

If you don't love her completely, let her go. If you're happier when she isn't around, let her go. If you're more interested in talking to other girls, let her go.

If you think you're doing her a favor by staying so you don't break her heart, you're wrong and an idiot.

Don't think you're doing her a favor by staying with her, because I can promise you that's not a favor. You're not easing her pain by trying to act happy in a relationship you're so desperately trying to get out of. You're not helping her by loving her out of guilt or obligation. **You're being selfish, and she deserves better than that.** I don't care who she is. If she's being loyal and loves you with her whole heart, she deserves better than that.

If you don't love the way she looks when she rolls out of bed in the morning, let her go. If you don't love the way she is when she's cranky and tired, let her go. If you don't love her when she's excited over the news she received over lunch, let her go. If you don't love the way she flirts with you and tries to make you happy, let her go. **Because she is every piece of that, every cranky, happy, and sad moment.** She is every imperfect and flawed part of her.

You can't chose the pieces of her you love because she is all of those tiny pieces made into one, and if you don't love her for those flawed pieces, you have to let her go.

Making her hold on when you have every intention of letting go isn't fair. It isn't fair to her for you to keep stringing her along. You're not saving her from a heartbrea. You're not making her feel better by staying with her out of pity, you're being selfish. All you're really doing is stopping her for finding someone who really and truly loves every part of her.

Someone will love the way she cries at sad movies. Someone will love her when she's had a tough day. Someone will love her when she's overly excited and can't control her happiness. Someone will love how she laughs like a fool when she's in a good mood. Someone will love the way she sleeps and look at her like she's his whole world.

No one is perfect. Everyone has bad days and bad attitudes, but you have to love them through their rough parts. Everything isn't going to be sunshine and rainbows. Relationships are hard and they require constant work and love. **If you can't picture a future with her through the hard parts, let her go.**

If you don't love every part of her don't stay with her out of guilt because you don't want to break her heart.

The only thing that is truly worse than being alone is being with someone who makes you feel alone, and that's what you're doing to her.

You're making her feel alone by not giving her love.

I'm not saying she's perfect, and I know there are things that drive everyone crazy about the people they care about, but you can't dissect those parts of her. You can't pick and pull at the pieces of her you don't love. You can't change her into the perfect person, and you shouldn't try. If you don't love every part of her, you need to let her go.

If she isn't your absolute best friend through the good and bad times, let her go. If you don't want to run to her with good news, let her go. If you don't want to take care of her when she's sick, let her go. **Let her go unless you want to love her,** *all over her,* **through the good, but especially through the bad.**

Don't stay with her because you're scared to break her heart while you're already out looking for someone new. You're a shitty person and she deserves better. She deserves someone who will love every piece of her, and that person is out there. Let her go so she can find the person whose heart throbs every time he sees her and is certain he wants to spend forever with her.

49

It's Pathetic How Much I Just Want To Hear From You

I can repeat over and over again how much I don't care about you. I can lie and tell my friends that I haven't thought about you and that I'm doing just fine without you. I can make empty promises that I don't miss you. I can convince myself every time my phone lights up that I'm not hoping your name will be showing up across my screen.

I wonder to myself what would happen if you messaged me. I slightly hope I'll hear from you with an apology, an explanation, something to give me a little peace of mind. But I don't know if I'll get that, ever.

I tell myself if you do message me I'll wait it out. Make you sweat, but at the same time I don't know if you will sweat. I don't know if you'll be worried at all because if you ask me, right now you're doing a damn good job of keeping the silence growing. I tell myself I won't answer you because maybe then you'll see how it feels.

But in all honestly, I think I'd only pretend to be stubborn and act annoyed to hear from you. I'd act like I can't believe you even bothered texting me after all this time, but secretly I'd be glowing on the inside. I'd almost feel relieved, like maybe you do actually care about me and maybe you do actually miss me too.

And I'd hate myself for admitting that.

I'd hate so much that I've let you have so much power over me.

I'd hate that just because you finally sent me a message, one you wouldn't even have to show up at my door and deliver, but a fucking message that only takes a few seconds to write would make me happy.

I should be angry. I shouldn't let a message do justice after days of not talking to me, just letting me go without an explanation. I should be annoyed to hear from you and your message shouldn't mean a thing, but it would. **It's pathetic how much I wish I would hear from you.**

I sit here all day trying to push thoughts of you out of my mind while you probably don't even think twice about me. I wonder over and over where I went wrong while you probably just found someone better. It's pathetic that if you messaged me, I'd try to play it coy and be short, but in all honestly my chest would be pounding waiting for your next response.

You go against everything I believe in, but what can I say?

There's something about you that does something to me. It makes it so hard to let you go and walk away.

I'll tell myself I won't chase after you because I won't. I won't blow up your phone; I won't send you question marks when you don't answer. **I won't make an effort to let you know I miss you, but I will miss you; I'll miss you from a distance.** I'll let the pain burn inside of me until the fire dies out and you're only a memory of what could have been.

It's pathetic how much I want to hear from you, but I won't

let you know how pathetic I really feel. So I'll keep my phone by my side and hope to God I'll see your name, but if not, it was nice to know you.

50

I Wanted You But I Don't Need You (So Don't Expect Me To Chase You)

I wanted you in a deep and almost desperate way. I wanted to find out where every scar and scab on your body came from. I wanted to know every story behind your tattoos. I wanted to know what was behind those blue of yours. I wanted to learn of your previous loves and what gets you out bed in the morning. I wanted to know what the future could hold for us, but there is no *us*. Not anymore.

Now there is only you and there is only me. We are separate again. We fell apart nearly as fast as we fell together.

I don't need you. I only wanted you. I won't run to you. I won't question why you just left. I won't blow up your phone or come running after you. That's not me, not anymore at least. If you don't want me anymore, that's your choice and I'll let you go. There is nothing I can say that will make you stay. There is nothing I want to say to change your mind.

You simply made the choice that I wasn't what you wanted, so you're free to go now, but you already knew that. I won't try to stop you.

I do miss you, though. I didn't think it would sting like this, but it does. It still stings and it still burns. I thought maybe it would be painless. After all, it feels like we barely knew each other now.

I've never woken up by your side, but every time I hear that stupid song you love so much on the radio I think of you. I've never cut your hair, but every time I see someone with curly brown hair coming my direction I secretly hope it's you. I've never seen you cry, but I still have to see that annoying heart next to your name to remind me of you every time I get on Snapchat.

There was so much more I wanted to learn from you and about you, so much more I wanted to give you. But there's no need now, because you decided it was over. It was just enough for you and you walked away.

I wouldn't give much, but I'd give a little something in order to run my fingers through your curly hair and kiss you on the mouth. I'd give a little something to hear your accent roll off your tongue and to help you plan your future trips that I secretly hoped I could become part of. I'd give a little something to roll on the floor with your dog and eat cheese pizza with you while you laugh telling me how plain that is.

But all those little something I'd give it still wouldn't be enough because I can't make you stay, and I don't want to try if I'm not what you want. I'll never try to make you stay and I'll never chase after you because I don't think the right person will have to be chased after.

I may want you, but I sure as hell don't need you.

I won't run after you to prove that I'm worth it because to you I wasn't, and that's all right. So I'll let you go, freely and peacefully, and if you come back I can't promise I'll be here.

About the Author

Becca Martin was born and raised in central New York. She's a writer who enjoys traveling, drinking margaritas, and attempting to take selfies with dogs. When she's not writing about the single life, she can often be found hanging out with friends and not flirting with boys because frankly it's just not something she's good at. Cheers to the single life!

Thought Catalog, it's a website.
www.thoughtcatalog.com

Social
facebook.com/thoughtcatalog
twitter.com/thoughtcatalog
tumblr.com/thoughtcatalog
instagram.com/thoughtcatalog

Corporate
www.thought.is

Printed in Great Britain
by Amazon